The Visitor's Guide to
BRITTANY

FRANCE

KEY FOR MAPS

Towns - Villages

Motorways

Main Roads

Country Boundary

County Boundary

Rivers

Canals

Railways

Lakes/Reservoirs

Museum/Art
Gallery/Centre

Cave

Archaeological Site

Building/
Country Park
Gardens

Castle/Fort

Ecclesiastical
Building

Wildlife Park/Zoo
Nature Reserve

Other Place
of Interest

Visitor's Guide Series

This series of guide books gives, in each volume, the details and facts needed to make the most of a holiday in one of the tourist areas of Britain and Europe. Not only does the text describe the countryside, villages, and towns of each region, but there is also valuable information on where to go and what there is to see. Each book includes, where appropriate, stately homes, gardens and museums to visit, nature trails, archaeological sites, sporting events, steam railways, cycling, walking, sailing, fishing, country parks, useful addresses — everything to make your visit more worthwhile.

Other titles already published or planned include:
The Lake District (revised edition)
The Peak District
The Chilterns
The Cotswolds
North Wales
The Yorkshire Dales
Cornwall
Devon
East Anglia
Somerset and Dorset
Guernsey, Alderney and Sark
The Scottish Borders
    and Edinburgh
The Welsh Borders
South and West Wales
The North York Moors,
    York and the Yorkshire Coast
Dordogne (France)
Black Forest (W Germany)
The South of France

The Visitor's Guide To
BRITTANY

Neil Lands

HUNTER
PUBLISHING INC

British Library Cataloguing in
Publication Data

Lands, Neil
    The visitor's guide to Brittany.
    1. Brittany (France) — Description
    and travel — Guide-books
    I. Title
    914.4'104838   DC611-B848

Illustrations have been provided by:
The French Government Tourist Office;
p13, 14, 15, 22, 26-7, 29, 30-2, 35, 39 (both),
41, 44, 47, 48 (lower), 50-1, 54-6, 58, 60, 63-
8, 70 (lower), 73, 83, 85, 87-9, 94, 96, 98-9,
118-19, 120, 121 (upper) 123-4, 126-7. Neil
Lands; p11, 19, 24, 28, 37-8, 40, 48 (upper),
61, 70 (upper), 76, 78, 82, 91, 93, 102, 109-
10, 114, 117, 121 (lower), 125. Illustration
on p17 supplied courtesy of Brittany
Ferries.

Colour illustrations were provided by:
Gernot (Coastline near Brest); Helen Race
(Mont St Michel); Lindsey Porter (Coastal
fishing, Pornichet, La Baule, St Nazaire); P.
Ploquin (Veryach, Château de la Bretesche);
Neil Lands (Fougerès Castle, Vitré Castle, The
coast of Brittany).

Published in the UK by
Moorland Publishing Co Ltd,
8 Station Street,
Ashbourne, Derbyshire,
DE6 1DE England.
Tel: (0335) 44486

ISBN 0 86190 108 8 (paperback)
ISBN 0 86190 109 6 (hardback)

Published in the USA by
Hunter Publishing Inc,
300 Raritan Center Parkway,
CN94, Edison, NJ 08818

ISBN 0 935161 22 8 (paperback)

Printed in the UK by
Butler and Tanner Ltd,
Frome, Somerset.

Contents

List of Illustrations

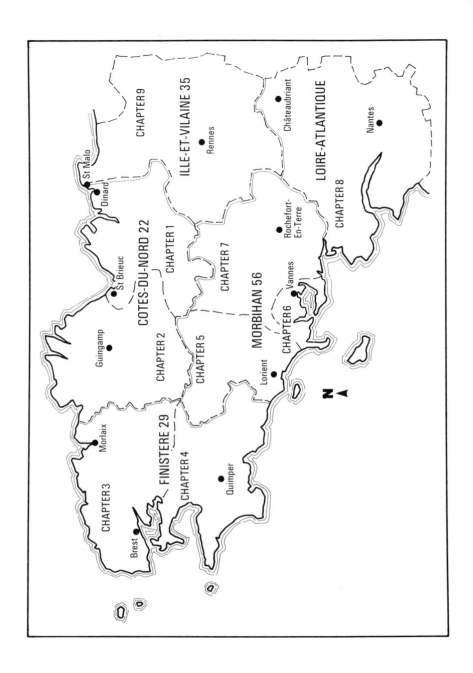

An Historical Introduction

In the little town of Dinan, up the narrow path which leads towards the ramparts from the river Rance, is the little park known as the English Garden.

Here, well concealed in the trees, stands the church of St Sauveur, where in a little chapel off the north aisle is a large stone slab bearing a curious inscription which may be roughly translated as follows:

> Here lies the heart of Messire Bertrand Duguesclin, sometime Constable of France who died on the 13th day of July 1380, and whose body lies with the Kings at St Denis, in France.

In *France, ie* elsewhere, you will note. Brittany, is, or was, therefore, somewhere apart from France, almost a separate country. This fact, if taken at face value, can come as a considerable blow to any devoted Francophile, for Francophilia is an infection to which even the French are not immune and one for which the only cure is more of the ailment.

But if Brittany is not France, should Francophiles even go there? Will it have what we seek and supply our wants in food, wine and ambiance? The answer, happily, is a firm 'yes' and no lover of France can fail to be charmed by this delightful and historic province.

Brittany is large. Today, strictly speaking, it embraces four *départements,* but we also include here the recently excised Loire-Atlantique which brings the true total to five, the other four being Finistère, Morbihan, Ille-et-Vilaine, and Côtes du Nord, where our travels will begin.

Brittany is famous for its coast. There are over seven hundred miles of it, embracing wide sandy beaches, rocky headlands, tall cliffs, innumerable islands, little coves, salt marsh and fens. We shall tour all around this coast, but you should go inland as well, to the 'Argoat', the 'country of wood', to give your travels variety as well as history. A traveller who visits only the coast misses a great deal.

The origins of Brittany's long history are truly 'wrapped in the mists of time', shrouded in legend, folklore and superstition. It is difficult to divide historical fact from ancient legend, and since it is all interesting one need not try too hard. Brittany is still a mysterious land and for many centuries was not even 'Brittany' at all. It is, at heart, a Celtic country, and the Celts came before the Gauls. Who these early people were, the people who built the megaliths of Finistère and erected the menhirs at Carnac, we do not really know. We do know that they were succeeded by the Gauls, who were divided, as elsewhere, into the various clans of a complex federation and called their land Armorica, 'the land facing the sea'.

In 56BC the Romans came, the legions of Caesar, to conquer and subdue the Gallic tribes, and those who would not submit, like the Veneti, were slaughtered, or sold into slavery. The Roman rule was relatively brief, and at this tip of their Empire the tribal names have often been preserved. The Veneti were from what is now Vannes, the Redones from Rennes, the Namnetes from Nantes and so on.

9

Crassus and Decimus Brutus conquered Armorica for Caesar, the one by land and the other by sea, Brutus destroying the Veneti fleet in the Gulf of Morbihan and, for the next four hundred years the Roman rule endured, before it in its turn crumbled before the advance of the Northmen. By this time the country was already Christian. Pagan religions and Druidic rites were swept away by the eloquence of a host of saints from Ireland and Wales, those Celtic saints with unusual names, who made their way to Brittany, not just in boats but on leaves, or floating stones, (or so we are told!).

As the first centuries of the Christian era wore on, this trickle of missionaries was vastly increased by refugees, as the Saxons began first to smother the outlying settlements in Ireland and then ravage the coasts of Britain, forcing those who lived there to flee abroad.

'If there were a hundred tongues in every head' wrote one monk at the time, 'they could not tell all we have endured from those valiant, wrathful, purely pagan people.'

The Saxons broke down the walls of the Roman Empire, and by the middle of the fifth century they were established in Britain and had either extinguished the Romano-Britons or forced them to flee. The people of Britain had to go somewhere, and, as their land had been taken by the Saxons, they resolved to conquer another in their turn.

About the year 400AD, Maximus, a Romano-British general, 'fitted out a great fleet and filled it with every armed warrior in Britain and went into the land that is called Armorica and made war upon the Gauls that lived there.'

This is the basis of the story of how the Britons came to Brittany, and it is probably untrue. Western Armorica had been peacefully infiltrated by the Britons for centuries and any 'invasion' was probably no more than the arrival of troops evacuated from outlying garrisons. However, this period saw the end of Armorica and the land came to be called 'Brittany' or 'little Britain'.

The Saxons soon followed, of course, but here they were resisted. The Britons, or perhaps they should now be called Bretons, really had nowhere else to go. The rest of what is now France was also under attack, from the Teutonic Franks and the Visigoths, but even as they settled in the country to the east and south, the Bretons became established in Brittany until, by the middle of the sixth century, their grip on the province was secure.

The earliest historian of the Franks was Gregory of Tours, and he relates how, in his time, at about the end of the sixth century, Brittany contained three 'Kingdoms' which warred against the Franks and each other. The Frankish king, Clovis, defeated the Bretons and, in Frankish terms, replaced their 'Kingdoms' with 'Counties'. Each Count continued to behave as a king, however, and refused to either acknowledge Frankish authority or pay taxes, and the early Merovingians were content to leave them well alone.

Charlemagne sent his paladin Roland to Brittany on a punitive expedition in 778, and in the following century, the Emperor, Louis the Pious, gave his Imperial support to the Count of Vannes, Nominoé, who defeated his rivals, conquered the entire province and held it as a subject king. After Louis's death, however, Nominoé threw off all his allegiance to the Carolingians, and his successors, the Counts of Brittany, fought the Franks and the Northmen for the next two hundred years.

In 939 the Breton Alain Barbe-Torte defeated the Normans, and Alain's descendants ruled Brittany as a quasi-independent state until 1488, paying little more than lip service to the King of France. At the end of this period, during the Hundred Years' War, Brittany was scourged by the War of the Breton Succession, when the rival houses of Blois and Montfort fought for the province and were supported, by the Kings of France and England, each hoping for the allegiance of the ducal house.

The feudal system is best regarded as a pyramid, the king at the top, linked by an interlocking series of allegiances to the peasant at the bottom. It was a system held together by self-interest. The lord promised protection and the subject promised obedience. In practice, however, there were many exceptions. The Kings of France, were, in theory, the overlords of all Frenchmen, and every French lord owed the king his obedience. In practice, such nobles as the Dukes of Brittany, Aquitaine and Burgundy and the Counts of Toulouse were independent sovereigns, who swore an oath of homage to the king on their accession and afterwards did exactly as they pleased. During the Middle Ages the French kings gradually destroyed these overmighty subjects, and brought the entire Kingdom under their actual, as opposed to theoretical, rule. The Counts of Toulouse were extirpated by the Albigensian Crusade in the thirteenth century. The Dukes of Aquitaine, who were usually also the Kings of England, were eventually defeated and dispersed, and the Dukes of Burgundy, after a hundred years of glory, conveniently died. By the end of the fifteenth century, only Brittany still held out as an independent power, and

The coat of arms of Anne of Brittany

then a combination of force and marriage finally brought the Duchy down.

You will not go far in Brittany before you see somewhere or something named after 'La Duchesse Anne', the last reigning sovereign of an independent Brittany.

As part of the treaty following a rebellion, Duke Francis II had promised that his children should not be married without the permission of the French King, but when he died in 1488, his daughter, Anne, married Maximilian of Austria. Maximilian had previously been married to Mary, daughter of the last Duke of Burgundy, Charles the Bold. The French King, Charles VIII, had no intention of being encircled by the House of Hapsburg, and marched an army into Brittany.

To complicate matters, Charles was the the time betrothed to Maximilian's daughter, Margaret, but in the end, all betrothals, marriages and arrangements were annulled, and Charles VIII of France married the Duchesse Anne of Brittany. Much to everyone's surprise, (including I suspect, their own,) they were very happy.

In 1499, however, Charles banged his head on a lintel in the château at Amboise and suddenly died. What followed is an intriguing example of medieval manoeuvres. All Anne's children by Charles had died, and the heir to the throne was Louis, Duke of Orléans, a friend of her father, who was therefore crowned as Louis XII. Louis was already married, but he, like Charles VIII, had no wish to lose control over the Breton duchy, and begged the Borgia Pope, Alexander VI, for an annulment, which was brought to Chinon by no less a person that Cesare Borgia himself, who obtained in return the services of a French army for the wars in Italy. The annulment obtained, Louis married his predecessor's widow!

In 1499 their daughter, Claude of France, was born; she was swiftly betrothed, at six years of age, to the heir to the throne, François d'Angoulême, the future Francis I. Anne's marriage agreement with Louis stated that Brittany would remain independent, but after Anne's death in 1514, the king prevailed on Claude to ignore this provision and bequeath the Duchy to the Dauphin Francis, before she in turn died, in 1524.

Francis I then persuaded the *parlement* of Brittany that their best long-term interests lay in union with France and in 1532, the Breton lords met at Vannes and requested the Royal favour, which was gladly granted by the King at Nantes later the same year. It was a decision with which not all Bretons are happy even today.

Brittany survived the ravages of the Hundred Years' War, the Wars of Religion and the Revolution better than most provinces but fell on rather harder times after the establishment of the Republic in 1789. A civil war against the Royalist, Catholic Bretons, or the *Chouans,* as they came to be called, raged in Brittany and the Vendée for many years. The period was marked by many atrocities, notably mass executions of Royalists at Rennes and Nantes, where thousands of prisoners were tied together and thrown into the Loire to drown.

In 1532, however, the French Crown had gained a formidable inheritance, a huge tract of land, a wolf's-head snarling into the Atlantic, and lordship over a tough race of people, good soldiers, and great seamen.

Le Conquet, Finistère

Brittany Today

Inland, Brittany is a rather uniform country of rolling hills and valleys, not mountainous, but never monotonous. Only in the Arrée 'mountains' which shelter the frontier of Finistère, are there any high hills and, apart from the Loire, there are few big rivers, but many creeks and inlets. The word that comes to mind again and again in Brittany is 'agreeable'. It really is, on all levels, a very agreeable place, and in many ways unique.

The Breton tongue is still spoken, although mainly by the older people, and the country has a tradition and a folklore quite divorced from that of France. Apart from the départements, and the difference between the *Armour* (the coast) and the *Argoat* (the hinterland), the country is also divided into 'Upper' and 'Lower' Brittany.

'Upper' Brittany lies inland to the east, and surprisingly, is in fact much less hilly than 'Lower' Brittany, which lies roughly west of a line between Vannes and St Brieuc. Breton is mostly spoken in 'Lower' Brittany, away from the language-polluting frontier with France, and it is here that travellers will see, more often than elsewhere, those lacey Breton *coiffes*. The *coiffes,* a feature of Breton dress, have a variety of shapes, of which the tall *Bigouden* is most familiar. These Breton costumes, like the language, are slowly dying out, and can now be seen only on the old people at fairs and on market days, sometimes at weddings, and, as a matter of custom and respect, at the Breton 'pardons'.

A 'pardon' is a procession, a pilgrimage, and nearly every Breton town has an annual pardon to the tomb of the local saint. The Bretons are a religious people, and their churches are

Breton ladies in coiffes

well preserved, full of curiosities and surprisingly large.

Their religious architecture also contains those surprising manifestations of religious fervour, the 'calvaries'. These, often used to typify Brittany, are in fact quite rare, and found mainly in Finistère, where they form the centrepiece in that other artistic phenomenon, the 'parish-close'.

Breton churches are also notable for fine steeples, belfried and bell towers, and from many examples I have selected some of the best to visit. I should explain here, that while this book covers the entire province, no attempt has been made to mention every town or village. There are many other places to be discovered which are not frequented by tourists but I have, I believe, included the best.

Quite apart from religion, but strongly linked with it in the past, is folklore. Brittany is the home of Sir Lancelot, of Morgan-le-Fay and the Lady of the Lake, of Druids, of wishing wells and magic fountains. We shall visit Brocéliande, and the haunts of Merlin and shall find, especially in the stories of the saints, that in Brittany, fact, legend and superstition are inextricably mixed. Brittany contains the largest number of megalithic remains in Western Europe, notably at Carnac, and in the north of Finistère; lovers of pre-history will find their passion fully indulged. But Brittany, the land of Armorica, remains the country of the sea.

Calvary at Pleyben

It is said, by the way of description, that Brittany is very like Cornwall, a land of cliffs and inlets, and this is very true. The entire coast is seamed with creeks and harbours, so that next to tourism, fishing is the major industry. The yachtsman has ousted the fisherman from many of his old haunts, and every tidal water now supports a flotilla of pleasure craft, which crowd these attractive, if dangerous, waters. Bénodet, in the south of Finistère, is just one of a hundred yachting centres, but one of the best.

Apart from modern pleasures, the country has ancient charms. Some of the towns, Dinan, Vannes, Vitré for example, are medieval gems, full of old, leaning buildings hovering over narrow cobbled streets. Others, equally ancient, were ravaged by bombing in World War II and have been rebuilt with some taste but little imagination. St Nazaire, Brest and Lorient are good examples of this. The largest city in the province is Nantes; even though now part of the neighbouring province of Pays de la Loire, it remains a large attractive Breton city of considerable charm.

Those who like castles should not fail to visit Vitré, Fougères, Josselin, or the later Vauban fortress of Port-Louis opposite Lorient. These still have their medieval or seventeenth-century walls intact and are well preserved, mighty castles, which would be fortresses even today. Those whose pleasure lies more at the table than in furious war, will be well

15

served in Brittany, *provided that they like sea food.*

The seas around the coast are, in every sense, bountiful. The lobsters of Camaret will lead a whole procession of crabs, langoustines, oysters, mussels, whelks and winkles on to your plate, all served in a variety of ways and all accompanied by the only Breton wine, Muscadet, or perhaps by cider. I have rarely eaten anywhere as well as in Brittany and never found a region where the standard of cooking is so consistently high and the cost of good eating so reasonable.

As to the weather, it rains; not to excess, but regularly. If the weather in Britain is wet, then you should head for the southern shore of Brittany and enjoy the Morbihan, while, if the summer in Britain is warm, the north coast of Brittany, the Côte d'Emeraude, has much to recommend it.

Brittany is popular with holiday-makers and is best visited out of season, away from the peak period, mid-July to early September. If you *must* go at that time, you must book ahead, especially if travelling through the more popular regions. Brittany is attractive out of season, particularly in May or June and during the month of October. The province is a paradise for birds, and therefore for birdwatchers, and these are the months when great flocks of seabirds can be seen at their best.

In this book I have tried to seek out the lesser known places and urge my readers to do so, following always the 'Three Principles for Happy Travelling in France', which are to travel on minor roads, to stay in *Logis de France* hotels,

and to eat at restaurants mentioned in the *Michelin Guide.*

Good maps are always useful and the whole region is covered in the Institut Geographique National Carte Touristique 1:250,000 No 5 *Bretagne.* I also rely, for good eating and comfortable hotels, on the *Gault-Millau Guide de la France,* and those places where I have had a particularly good meal are mentioned in this book.

So much then, for the history and the places. But what of the people? They too, have a history.

St Malo, which is visited first, as a terminal port for Brittany Ferries, is said to have produced more famous sons than any other town in France.

Brittany has a score of notable names to look back on: knights like Bertrand Duguesclin, who harried the English up and down France, explorers and navigators like Cartier and Surcouf, soldiers like Cambronne, writers like Châteaubriand and Jules Verne, lovers like Abélard, Ernest Renan, philologist, historian and philosopher. All were Bretons, and justly proud of their origin.

Those who travel round this large and agreeable province will find many traces of these people and their past. The Bretons' instinct is to preserve their history and traditions, and resist the new, if newness is all that there is to recommend it. Brittany is a French province, but one with its own distinct and special flavour. It is very like certain parts of England, and it takes time for the traveller to absorb that exciting 'foreign' feeling, but, be sure, it will come.

Travel

Air France offer flights between Paris and major international cities such as New York or London. Air Inter is the national domestic airline. There are internal flights between Paris and Rennes, Dinard, Saint-Brieuc, Lannion, Brest, Quimper, Lorient and Nantes. Many of these flights now connect with Air France's international service.

France has many car-hire agencies, and fly-drive arrangements are available through airlines and tour operators.

Rail services from Paris are by fast train to major towns. French Railways operate regular bus services between the major resorts and the stations; other bus services are few.

Brittany is well served with cross-Channel ferries. Brittany Ferries sail daily from Portsmouth to St Malo, and from Plymouth and Cork to Roscoff. For the Côtes-de-Nord and Ille-et-Vilaine *departements,* the port of Cherbourg offers a shorter sea crossing, and a direct route south, down the Cotentin peninsula, bringing the traveller into Brittany across the river from Mont-St-Michel.

Brittany Ferry

1 The Côtes-du-Nord: St Malo to St Brieuc

St Malo, city of corsairs! Coming in from the sea, even the seascape of St Malo is distinctly menacing. The ship weaves its way carefully through a maze of rocks and reefs, threading a course from lighthouse to lighthouse. Coming in at night, the approach is made through a network of flashing red, green and white lights, all over-towered by the regular glare from the lighthouse on the heights of Cap Fréhel, to the west.

From earliest times until the end of the Napoleonic Wars, these reefs were the first bastion protecting the raiding craft of St Malo from summary justice at the hand of the British Navy. During the sixteenth and seventeenth centuries in particular, few vessels in the Channel could escape paying tribute to the privateers who sailed from St Malo and took their ships and plunder home again to a safe harbour in the Rance, under the guns of St Malo and the Tour Solidor.

As you sail in, the town itself, St Malo

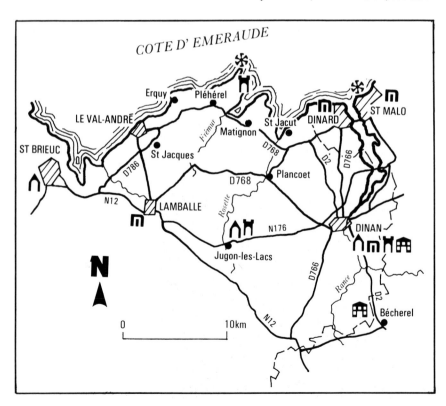

Inter-Muros, lies snugly to the left, behind high ramparts. It looks the archetypal Vauban fortress, but this ancient appearance is in some ways deceptive.

The old fortress town and port of St Malo was obliterated in World War II when, after the Normandy invasion of 1944, the German commander withdrew inside the walls and defied the American Army to evict him. The siege of St Malo lasted two weeks, during which time the fortress was pounded by field artillery and the guns of the British Fleet. When the Germans eventually surrendered, old St Malo was a wreck.

However, the *Malouins,* the people of St Malo, are a tough, resilient crowd and they decided to rebuild their city in the old style; what you see to-day is a city reconstructed in styles ranging from medieval up to the eighteenth century, with the more useful twentieth-century additions of good lighting, smooth streets and mains drainage, which make a stay more pleasant.

The port is busy and the fishing fleet still sails, as always, for the cod-banks off Iceland. The sea is the true work place for the people of St Malo and many great French seamen have sailed from under her walls.

In the sixteenth century, Jacques Cartier sailed to Newfoundland, but discovered the wide estuary of the great St Lawrence. Cartier thought he had

The museum and town hall, St Malo

19

arrived in Cathay, like Marco Polo, rather than in America, but when he met Indians along the river, he took their name for the word 'village' — Canada — to be the name of their country and possessed the land for the French King, a step which eventually led to conflict with England and the Seven Years' War.

Another great colonizer from St Malo was Mahé La Bourdonnais, who explored the Indies. A more warlike and yet tragic figure is Porçon de la Bardinais, who commanded a St Malo frigate guarding French shipping against the Barbary pirates, was captured and taken to Algiers. He would normally have been sent to row out his life on the galleys, but the Bey of Algiers sent him to Louis XIV with peace proposals, charging him to return to imprisonment if the proposals were rejected. They were, and in blunt terms, but Porçon kept his word and carried the king's harsh answer back to Algiers, where it so enraged the Bey that he had Porçon blown to pieces at the cannon's mouth. An unpleasant end was the frequent fate of St Malo's sailors, for they were inveterate pirates, and even the king's commission or *letter of marque* could not always convince their captors that their raids were legitimate.

A host of pirates, privateers, navigators, and corsairs sailed from St Malo, the difference between each category being rather obscure, especially to their victims, but their lust for plunder and adventure took them far afield. Surcouf, for example, ravaged the East India Company's ships on the trade routes to the Indies, and did so well that he retired a rich man before he was forty.

A hundred years before Surcouf, between 1673 and 1736, René Duguay-Trouin, harassed the Channel shipping and even landed men to raid the coast of England. These men and a host of others lived from the sea and enriched the city from their spoils. They are commemorated at the town's museum at the St Vincent Gate.

A taste of a vanished, but more recent, *Malouin* way of life can be found at the Hotel Univers on the Place Châteaubriand, where the bar is decorated with paintings, ship's models, and old photographs, all recording the great days of St Malo and the sea, in times more peaceful than those of the corsairs.

The *Inter-Muros* is completely encircled by the repaired twelfth-century ramparts, buttressed here and there with towers and *glacis,* decorated with statues of the town's great men and with fine views over the sea approaches. If you look down into the streets you can also see, under the walls, some of the town's fine restaurants, notably La Duchess Anne, the Auberge de l'Hermine or the Central in the Grande Rue, where you will get a very warm welcome.

Moving around the ramparts you will come eventually to Beaufils' statue of Châteaubriand, another son of St Malo, who was almost born on the little island of La Grande Bé, which lies just off the port, in September 1768. His mother, who must have become bored with waiting, had decided to go for a row in a small boat. She went into labour when they arrived at La Grande Bé, and the party hurriedly returned to St Malo, where René was born within a few hours.

René de Châteaubriand spent most of his boyhood in St Malo, went to school in Dinan, and at other times lived with his parents in their gloomy château at Combourg. The family, although noble, were not over-blessed with money, and in an effort to restore their fortunes, his father took up ship-owning, the only

PLACES OF INTEREST AROUND ST MALO

Fort La Latte
25km (15 miles) west on the Fréhel cape. A medieval fortress, very spectacular.

Dinan
22km (14 miles) south, on the river Rance. A very fine town, with medieval buildings and a great castle, the home town of Bertrand du Guesclin.

Castle Museum, Dinan
A display of weapons and local folklore.

Tour Solidor
On outskirts of St Malo beside the Rance, a fifteenth-century tower built to guard the shipping.

Cancale
Attractive fishing port 35km (21m) east, towards Mont St Michel on the coast road, famous for oysters.

Quic-en-Groigne Tower
St Malo Inter-Muros.

Le Grande Bé
A small island, just off the ramparts of St Malo, only open across the causeway at low tide. The grave of René de Châteaubriand is on the north side.

Combourg
Situated 30km (19 miles) south-east of St Malo, this castle was the birthplace and family home of Châteaubriand.

occupation open to a gentleman under the *Ancien Regime* which did not involve the loss of his patent of nobility. The venture was reasonably successful, and his son therefore enjoyed the benefits of an expensive education.

René tried various careers, including the army and diplomacy, but he began to write at twenty-two, and continued to do so until his death at the age of eighty. The French often refer to Châteaubriand as their greatest writer, mainly on account of his style. This is charitable from the nation that has produced Hugo, Zola, Balzac, and Voltaire, to name but a few and especially so since Châteaubriand's style is, in the main, gloomy, probably the result of the unhappiness of his private life. His major work, *Memoires d'Outre-Tombe*, 'Memories from Beyond the Grave' is a typical example.

His childhood was depressing, his marriage disastrous, his ambition consuming. He was not a happy man. At the end of his life he asked the people of St Malo for 'six feet of rock' on the Grande Bé, and there, on the island where he was so very nearly born, he was buried in 1848.

St Malo has now long outgrown the walls and is a well-developed port and holiday resort. Most of the hotels are in the suburb of Paramé, to the east, and the Hotel Alba in the Rue des Dunes, which overlooks the bay is particularly recommended.

St Malo is today, a cheerful, bustling town and, like most seaports, an exciting place to visit. It has an aquarium with a host of Channel fish, some of quite alarming aspect, and a fine museum in the old castle with relics of the corsairs. There are numerous walks outside the town to the forts and, at low tide, even across the causeway to Le Grand Bé. Châteaubriand's tomb, under a massive

The beach at Dinard

granite cross, is on the seaward side, looking out to the ocean, and away from the little town which, as he himself remarked, has as fine a record for famous men as any town in France.

Opposite St Malo lies Dinard, in complete contrast; quiet, Edwardian, elegant, almost refined. It may be reached from St Malo by the cross-harbour ferry. In a different world from St Malo, the town could describe itself as the 'Pearl of the Côte de'Emeraude', for Dinard, let it be said, has style.

About 1870, when just a little port, it was 'discovered' by the British and Americans. Coming first to visit, and then to settle, these strangers set their mark on the former port and it remains after much building and re-building, Edwardian in aspect and extremely popular. The town greatly resembles Torquay in Devon, especially from the walk around the Pointe de Moulinet.

Dinard has large hotels, a casino, excellent beaches, a huge indoor swimming pool, built at vast cost some twenty years ago, and some excellent and expensive restaurants, notably the Roche-Corneille and, more typically and less costly, the quaintly-named Petit-Robinson. Dinard has panache. In summer it is thronged with a lively and well-dressed crowd and it reminds one of childhood holidays in Devon, of sand and rock pools, of walks along the cliffs, of fishing nets and seaweed, chasing crabs and endless hours spent trying to prise shellfish off the rocks.

On the right bank of the Rance, down across the estuary, may be seen the high bulk of the Tour Solidor, built by Jean IV in 1382 to overawe the *Malouins,* a vain task, in view of their intransigent reputation. It now contains the Musée des Cap-Horners, dedicated to the days of the clipper ships and a most interesting place to visit, while the Hôtel de la Rance nearby is a good place for lunch.

My favourite town in the Côtes-du-Nord is Dinan, an old walled town of 20,000 inhabitants, with red flowers against golden walls, battlements and leaning houses built above the Rance. Many days could be spent in Dinan, exploring the town on foot, or foraying out into the nearby countryside, but one should go first to the main square, the Place de Guesclin and have a *kir* at a table outside the Hôtel Avaugour. To be exact, the Avaugour is in the Place du Champ-Clos, but the difference is minimal since the two are only separated by a low wall.

Dinan is the home-town of the knight, Bertrand Duguesclin, Fabian General and sometime Constable of France. His equestrian statue may be seen from outside the Avaugour, though closer inspection reveals that, whatever his personal and military qualities, Bertrand was not over-burdened with good looks. He was, in fact, downright ugly.

Bertrand was born at La Motte Broom castle, north of Dinan, then a possession of the Duke Jean III. Knighted in 1356, the year of Poitiers, he entered the French King's service at a time when the king himself was a captive in England. Meanwhile, the War of the Breton Succession was raging, and in 1359 Duguesclin occupied Dinan with a small force and held it against an English army under John, Duke of Lancaster. During the siege, Bertrand was challenged to single combat by an English knight, Sir Thomas Canterbury, and promptly accepted. The combat took place between the armies in what is now the Champ-Clos. Canterbury was left dead upon the field; dead, but not entirely forgotten; there is a Canterbury Restaurant just opposite the Champ-Clos in the Rue Ste Clair, where the food

Betrand Duguesclin, Dinan

is memorable.

Duguesclin fought the English for the next sixteen years and he was not always so successful. He was captured at Auray, ransomed, then captured again at the Battle of Najéra in Spain, and yet again at Juigne, but in the end Duguesclin's Fabian tactics wore the English down. Duguesclin liked the English, and always enjoyed his periods of captivity in the English Court, for he was never kept in prison. Many of the English knights, notably John Chandos and Robert Knollys, were his personal friends. He merely wanted the English to stay on their own side of the Channel, a widely-shared sentiment at the time, and indeed later.

For their part, the English admired Bertrand immensely and took a great interest in his welfare. When he was unhorsed at Auray and in danger of death, John Chandos rode to his rescue through the press and persuaded him to surrender his sword, saying: 'Come now, Bertrand, give up your sword. This day cannot be yours, but there will, cértes, be another'.

Bertrand's wife, the beautiful and mysterious Tiphanie, who was said to have second sight, and might, but for Bertrand's reputation, have been burned as a witch, also came from Dinan, and when Bertrand himself was dying outside the walls of Châteauneuf, he expressed the wish to be buried at his home on the Rance, in the town of his boyhood.

From the Champ-Clos, make for the old Keralty *maison* in the Rue Léhon, a fine sixteenth-century house, which now contains the *Syndicate d'Initiative*. Its staff will provide a variety of information and a map of the town.

The Tour de l'Horloge, just ahead, was presented to the town by Duchesse Anne in 1507 and overlooks the Vieille Ville, the old *bourg*. The centre, the Place des Merciers, has fifteenth-century houses leaning wearily towards each other, and leads down to the steep and beautiful Rue de Jerzual, which itself makes a trip to Brittany worthwhile.

The sixteenth-century houses along the Rue Jerzual are beautifully preserved, their window-boxes crammed with geraniums on every ledge. The fortunate occupants are mainly artists, engaged in pottery, weaving, ironwork, painting or scuplture. This street leads down steeply to the encircling walls and the Rue du Petit-Ford. Dinan was once a port, and the banks of the Rance at the **Vieux-Pont are overlooked by a high** viaduct. A footpath leads up from the viaduct to the so-called 'English Garden' behind the *basilica* of St Sauveur, which contains, as noted in the introduction, the heart of Duguesclin who died of a fever in 1380 while besieging Châteauneuf-de-Randon in the Midi. The body went to St Denis, but his heart, in death as in life, belonged to Dinan. The *basilica,* built about 1120 in a mixture of styles, has some fine glass and sculpture, as well as a curious monument to St Roch, who freed the town from the plague in the sixteenth century. The church windows show the saints being martyred and the trades of which they are now the patrons.

In the town is the school where Châteaubriand was educated, and the great château, now a museum of Breton dress, is on the south-west rampart. Palm trees flourish in the old moat, an indication of the mild climate. The fortress itself is well worth a visit, as indeed are the old walls.

The castle was built rapidly between 1382 and 1387. The mercenery Oliver de Clisson was based here and scourged the country with his *routiers*. The Duchesse Anne herself sheltered here in 1507, giving the town the Tour Horloge in thanks for its hospitality.

In 1446, Gilles, the younger son of Duke Jean was imprisoned in the castle dungeon, apparently for arguing with his brother Duke François. It must have been a considerable quarrel, because after being starved and beaten, the young prince was finally strangled by the jailors. The castle is well preserved, an excellent example of a late medieval fortress.

On the other side of the town lies the Clôitre des Cordeliers, another building with a grisly tale to tell. Jean de Montfort, who after Auray became Duke Jean IV, visited the town in 1378 and found to his rage that the Franciscan monks of les Cordeliers still had a portrait of his dead rival, their patron Charles of Blois, on the wall. He ordered it to be removed, but when the monks did so, the wall behind it began to bleed, a spectacle which so horrified the duke that he fled from the town.

A pleasant excursion from Dinan is to descend any morning to the old port on the Rance and take one of the motor-boats which ply along the river between St Malo and Dinan — a trip of about two hours.

This is by far the best way to see the Rance, for no road directly overlooks it. The river winds along the steep wooded valley, gradually widening as it nears the grand *barrage*. This is not just a dam, but a tidal power-station. When the tide flows in, the turbines turn. When the

Château de Dinan

tide retreats, the pent-up water behind
the dam pours out after it, and so the
turbines turn again. As the world's first
hydro-electric dam, opened in 1967, it is
as close to perpetual motion as the world
has yet devised, and is open to visitors.

The boat returns to Dinan, the
junction for all the roads in this part of
the province, and from Dinan one can
tour out in all directions, either on foot,
for this is great walking country, or by
car, or, better still, by cycle.

Léhon, a suburb of Dinan, is famous
locally for its medieval cloister and for
the calvary of St Esprit, erected in 1359
by John of Gaunt, Duke of Lancaster,
whose troops were besieging the town.
The cloister is also the mausoleum of the
Beaumanoir family, of ancient Breton
stock. This stands on the remains of a
chapel built by Nominöe, the first King
of Brittany. The walk to Léhon from
Dinan, past the viaduct over the Rance,
makes an ideal evening stroll.

To the south, just within the Côtes-du-Nord, the département with which we are presently concerned, lies the fortress of Caradeuc. Almost always in Brittany the fortresses lie in the periphery of regions, designed to defend rather than oppress the inhabitants, and so it is here, although the present buildings are not particularly old.

Caraduec, twenty kilometres south of Dinan, built on an ancient site, dominates the road to Rennes. The present château was built about 1776 by Louis-René de Châlotais, who, as Procurer of Rennes defended the rights of the Breton *parlement* against the ever-

Dinan centre

enroaching central power of Paris.
Nearby lies the village of Becherel, a
walled little place of considerable charm,
with great wide views north towards
Dinan. East of Bécherel, lies Tinteniac, a
village full of flowers.

To the west of Dinan, past Jugon,
which has the oldest church in Brittany
and a castle, one should press on west, to
the old Penthièvre township of
Lamballe, a typical Breton township,
with whitewashed houses littered along a
ridge and the usual large church or
churches. All Breton churches seem too
large for any possible congregation, a
tribute to the religious life of the
community.

Lamballe, once the capital of the
Counts of Penthièvre, one of the great
Breton lordships, stands above the
Gouessant River, one of the minor but
attractive streams which flow north to

the Channel, across the Val-André.

At this point we veer east, to start a
tour along the coast, back to the Côte
d'Emeraude, which is reached at little St
Jacut, west of Dinard, but one cannot
escape from the sea for long in Brittany.
The Bretons share with the British a
national reluctance to see a piece of
water without a boat floating on it, and
every road seems to lead eventually to
the waterside.

The Côte d'Emeraude is jagged.
According to the map it runs from
Granville through St Cast to the wide
sandy beaches of Sables d'Or-Les-Pins.
This indented coastline is full of little
ports, villages and holiday resorts,
perfect for family holidays, and all very
much the same.

Dominating the Côte, however, is Cap
Fréhel, itself dominated by a great
lighthouse, which flashes its welcome

and warning far to the right as you sail in on the dark dawn towards St Malo. It is said that the light can be seen 70 miles away when the weather is good, and only 200 yards away when it is bad, an indication of the weather on this part of the coast!

The cape's colourful cliffs are nearly 300ft high, in dull pinks and greys, and on a fine day the contrast between the rose-coloured rocks, the white surf and the blue sea is startling, while below the cliffs, thickly clustered on the rocks, nest a host of seabirds. Gulls, terns and cormorants all swoop and soar over the waves, their cries piercing the dull boom and crash of the waves far below. You can view these cliffs by sea, on an excursion from Dinard, but from any angle, Cap Fréhel is the dominating feature of the Emerald coast.

To the south-east of the cape, across the Anse (or Bay) of Sévignes lies the fortress of La Latte. This is imposing even at a distance and grows in stature as it is approached.

La Latte was built by the pirate family of Goyon-Matignon in the Middle Ages and restored by Vauban in the seventeenth century. A menhir, or standing stone, called Gargantua's Finger, guards the landward approach, but La Latte is truly magnificent when viewed from the sea. In France a château can be any large country home, but a fortified castle is a *château-fort.* La Latte has all the attributes of a *château-fort;* the cliffs protect the seaward side. From the land, a double crevasse spanned by two drawbridges makes another natural defence, before you reach the fortress. This, behind a double *enceinte,*

Low tide, Erquy

Fort la Latte

contained a cannon-ball factory and barracks for a hundred men-at-arms. Visited in late evening, when the sun is plunging down the western sky behind Fréhel, La Latte is a fearsome place.

Further along the coast, reached by a series of narrow roads which overlook wide, white, sandy beaches, each of which will tempt you to stop, is the resort of Erquy. Here are no fewer than seven beaches, wide, clean expanses of sand being uncovered as the tide goes out.

Beyond these beaches, directly north

of Lamballe, and protected from the winds by Cap Fréhel on one side and the Tréguier peninsula on the other, Val-André is a mild, sheltered region of white sand beaches backed by pine woods. Away from the beach are the moated château at Bienassis, and the chapel of Notre-Dame-du-Bon-Voyage at St Jacques, but it is the sea-scapes which make the greatest impact on this part of the Côtes.

West of Val-André lies a vast bay, the Anse d'Yffiniac, stretching between Val André and the Pointe du Roselier, itself

Sables d'Or

inside the even larger bay of St Brieuc. A minor road leads close to the shore here and the views across the bay, especially a low tide, seem almost endless.

Finally we arrive at St Brieuc, whose traffic jams are a deterrant to the modern traveller.

It is quite easy to circle St Brieuc for some time, unable to penetrate the centre and find the Hôtel Beauregard. This is largely because St Brieuc's roads span two ravines by means of two viaducts. The town centre is dominated by the cathedral of St Stephen, begun in the thirteenth century; it has been burned,sacked, pillaged and generally damaged until as recently as 1944. However, even here, is a typical Breton surprise; unlike many Breton churches, St Stephen's, or rather to give it the French name, St Etienne, is quite small. In the chancel lies the sanctuary of St William, and the cathedral was once fortified and then severely battered during the War of the Breton Succession.

Legend has it that the first Bretons to arrive in Armorica, among them St Brieuc, all fleeing from the Northmen, landed near what is now St Brieuc, in the fifth century AD. They came ashore near Russe-de-Bréha, and must have found the country around St Brieuc, the so-called *Göelo,* quite delightful.

In late autumn, the countryside glows with the tall yellow gorse and purple heather, red cider apples blazing on the trees, and the landscape leaps to life as the sun comes out and illuminates the blue sea and the hills behind with a red evening glow. One should leave St Brieuc to view this colourful scenery, perhaps stopping for dinner at La Vieille Tour at Sand-La-Tour by the bay.

Dinan

The coast of Brittany

2 The Côtes-du-Nord: The Granit Rose Coast & Tregor

Past St Brieuc, the coast swings north towards the Tréguier peninsula, the 'ears' of the Breton wolf's head, but before heading north for more of these delightful bays and to provide a balance to the Breton scene, we turn south, for a brief visit to the towns of Montcontour and Quintin.

Montcontour is in the Penthièvre district and the central square, the Place de Penthièvre, is a perfect example of early eighteenth-century architecture. The town, on a steep hillside, was once completely walled, but apart from the architecture the real reason for coming here is to visit the little chapel of Notre-Dame-du-Haut. The key is kept at the farm to the right of the porch, but inside there is a delightful surprise.

Breton churches are often quite different from those in other parts of France. The Wars of Religion and the Revolution of 1789 did irreparable damage to the former glories of French religious art and architecture. Many churches were sacked, burned or secularized, congregations dispersed, windows smashed, statues defaced or decapitated. Unlike most English parish churches, which are homely affairs, often smelling of flowers and beeswax, the typical French church is today a bare, gloomy place, echoing eerily, a pale shadow of some former glory. There are exceptions here and there, but most French churches are depressing, and the visitor can and should be highly selective in those he chooses to look at.

Breton churches are different. Quite apart from the architecture, which is itself unique, they are full of interest, colour, and fascinating relics. A travel writer usually has to try hard to prevent his book from being a tour in and out of church doors, and from a host of churches select only his personal favourite, but in Brittany at least, the choice is wide and Notre-Dame-de-Haut is a good example.

Notre-Dame contains six statues to the 'healing' saints. St Mamar cures colic, which is unfortunate since he indicates his power by exposing his entrails. St Léon cures rheumatism, while St Meen is efficacious for nerves. St Hubert gives protection from the bites of mad dogs, St Houarniaule can be invoked against fear, while St Eugénie cures headaches!

Quintin lies to the west, another little town where the church contains the shrine for another pilgrimage, Notre-Dame-de-Delivrance, much prayed to by expectant mothers, and containing a reliquary with a piece of the Virgin's girdle. Quintin stands on, or rather overlooks, the Gouët River, one of a small network of local rivers all flowing north and east towards St Brieuc, but we go north, past Châtelaudren, back to the coast by the port at Binic, a fishing port, with a colourful fleet of trawlers, on a wide bay. The coast road runs up to St Quay and then on to Plouha, a significant stop. Here, and if not today then certainly until quite recently, this was regarded as the boundary between the French and Breton languages, for, from now on, as we travel across the old districts of Göelo, Trégor and Finistère, we are in a region where Breton is the language of the country and the people, which they speak at home and among themselves. Breton is now in slow retreat, or perhaps it is more exact to say at low ebb. The tide does appear to have turned and the local people are actively concerned with their identity as Bretons and their linguistic heritage, and interest in Breton music, language and folklore has never been higher.

Plouha is coping well with the onslaught of tourism, and is a trim, neat little place. Many of the Plouha cottages are owned by old naval pensioners, who keep their cottages suitably smart, and grow very succulent vegetables in the kitchen gardens. Going north, on the left of the Paimpol road, lies the little chapel of Kermaria, in yellow stone, a shady

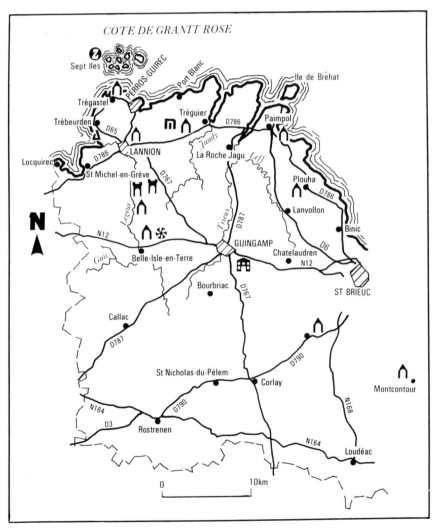

COTE DE GRANIT ROSE

place with a porch full of saints and containing a medieval 'Doom'. A 'Doom' is a vision of the Last Judgement; examples are becoming increasingly rare.

The chapel dates from the fourteenth century and the Doom here, which takes the form of a Dance of Death, was installed about 1450. All manner of folk are seen being hurried to Hell, and a scroll on a doleful note reminds us to:

. . . Leave all your pride
. . . You are not alone
. . . For all of your riches
. . . The richest has only a shroud

In some ways the Bretons seem preoccupied with death. Perhaps it is just that as a seafaring people they have seen a lot of it, but it appears as a theme in many of their artistic works. At least they do not seem afraid of it.

The coast above Plouha is extremely jagged, broken into a series of peninsulas, the first of whch contains Paimpol. This fairly typical Breton town, notable for a pleasant central square and the Relais Brenner, on the Pont-Lezardrieux, has served as the setting for books by Loti. Further up the peninsula is the Pointe de l'Arcouest and the ferry for the little isle of Bréhat, the largest of a score or more which lie off this coast.

Brittany is surrounded by islands, and it would take a lifetime to visit them all, but Bréhat is very pretty and, weather permitting, this is a short and pleasant

Cathedral of Tréguier

trip. The rocks there are really red, and the little gardens on the island are crammed with flowers and fig trees.

Beyond Paimpol, to the west via the bridge over the Trieux estuary, is Tréguier. The bridge spans a gorge which the locals call a *ria,* a word more commonly found on the north coasts of Spain, where it means 'estuary'. Further west, in Léon, they call these inlets *abers,* a word probably derived from Cornish or Welsh. Such links with Celtic Britain are found everywhere in Brittany.

Tréguier is an interesting place and worth a visit, especially the church, or rather the cathedral, of St Tudwal (or St Tugwell); his name sounds Cornish, and according to legend St Tudwell came from Britain and was a relative of King Arthur.

St Tudwal's cathedral contains, and rightly venerates, the tomb of St Yves. His head is kept in a reliquary in the sacristy. He is the patron saint of lawyers and their clients, and unlike some saints whose life and works are shrouded in legend, he definitely existed. He was born near Tréguier in 1253 and studied law in the Schools of Paris. He took Holy Orders in 1285 at Orleans, and then went to serve the Bishop of Renes, arguing cases in the Ecclesiastical Court, where he rapidly became very unpopular. He would not take bribes; he demanded the truth, and refused to favour the rich. After a stormy career, Yves died in 1303 and was instantly admitted to sainthood. It is interesting that by his tomb lies a plaque placed there by a group of American lawyers, who clearly found it necessary to come a very long way to seek the intercession of their own particular saint. His feast day is 19 May.

St Tudwal's also contains the tomb of Duke John V, who died in 1442. His tomb, and that of St Yves, are recent replacements, the originals having been destroyed in the Revolution. The church tower, incidentally, called the Hastings Tower, dates from the twelfth century.

Tréguier is an agreeable town in which to spend a day, perhaps visiting the house of Renan, the agnostic writer and philosopher, born here in 1823, or examining the half-timbered houses in the centre, or heading downhill to the quay for a drink at the little Café du Port. There are many interesting places around Tréguier, apart from the imposing coastline.

The recently restored castle at La Roche-Jagu has splendid views, while to the north lies the quaint little port of Porz-hir. A little way south lies St Yves' birthplace at Minihy-Tréguier. The church there stands on the site of his former home and in the churchyard is a medieval arched monument, under which pilgrims to St Yves are supposed to crawl on their knees. St Yves would probably not approve, although at Jaudy, petitioners to the saint had a much more complicated ritual to undergo, which included throwing a handful of nails through a window, entering the church backwards, and then shouting their request loudly to gain attention!

If you like quiet little places Port Blanc on the coast north of Tréguier, minute and calm, is ideal. When the tide is out it exposes an encircling reef, and a harbour, or bay, full of jagged rocks. Port Blanc has two good hotels, the Hôtel des Iles and the Grand, the former in fact, being the grander.

From the dining room at the Grand, it is interesting to watch the bay change shape and character as the tide comes in. If the day is calm and there are no waves, then the remorseless rising of the water is both eerie and beautiful. Watching the making and ebbing of the tides can become a daily pre-occupation in Brittany, almost mesmeric as the rocks slowly submerge and the beach imperceptibly narrows. The action of the tides in Brittany governs the day. The tide flows in, or 'floods' for about six-and-a-half hours, and remains steady, or 'slack water', for a brief period before it 'ebbs' or flows out again. The ebb takes as long as the flood, and there are two tides a day. Each day the time of high tide will be about an hour later than the previous day, and every month there are Spring and Neap tides. (A Spring tide is one with the highest high tides and the lowest low tides, while a Neap tide had the reverse; lowest high and highest low.)

The Grand at Port Blanc, just opposite the tiny little chapel of the Virgin atop its rock, is well worth a visit, for the welcome is warm, the Muscadet chilled, the food good and the prices reasonable. It even has Breton specialities such as the *Tom-ha-ynn*, a crêpe with ice-cream filling, covered with chocolate sauce, and finally flambéd in Grand-Marnier.

The coast road from Port Blanc to Tréburden stays right by the sea, past Perros-Guirec and Trégastel-Place, a very picturesque place with its blue-turreted castle on a rock, and our first *Plou* or parish — Ploumanac'h. From Ploumanac'h keen birdwatchers can take a trip to the bird sanctuary of the

Gateway to Tréguier

PLACES OF INTEREST ON THE GRANIT ROSE COAST AND TREGOR

Notre Dame-de-Haut, Montcontour
18km (11 miles) south of St Brieuc, this little village has a chapel of the 'healing' saints, six statues good for whatever ails you.

Treguieur
The tomb of St Yves, in St Tudwals Cathedral, is worth a visit. Open every day.

Beauport Abbey
5km (3 miles) south of Paimpol. Magnificent thirteenth-century ruins in attractive countryside.

The Sept Iles
A group of islands, all seabird sanctuaries off the Granit-Rose coast. Trips by boat from Perros-Guirec leave daily at 2pm, returning at 6pm.

The Ménez-Bré
26km (16 miles) west of Guingamp. A high hill with magnificent views over coast and countryside.

Trégastel
19km (11 miles) west of Tréguier. A fine seaside resort on the Granit Rose coast with a good beach and red rocks.

Port Blanc chapel

Ploumanac'h

Perros-Guirec

Sept Iles five miles offshore. One cannot land, but the seabirds are there in their thousands, and include auks and gannets, plunging fearlessly into the sea.

Ploumanac'h is attractive, very rocky, with an old customs' patrol path, the *sentier des douaniers,* now serving walkers as an enjoyable trek over to Perros-Guirec. This is a popular seaside resort, with a fine safe beach and an interesting port.

This is a smugglers' coast and further evidence of this lucrative, if rather risky, activity, can be found at the chapel of Our Lady at La Clarté, built on the highest point, to guide ships to safety in fog or bad weather — and who but smugglers would close this coast in fog?

Beyond La Clarté, up a side road towards the Telecommunications Centre, is a huge upright stone: the menhir of St Duzec.

Many menhirs, especially the large, solitary and imposing ones, were the site of pagan rites before the Christian era. Too big to be moved, the early missionaries turned these objects into Christian shrines, and after due exorcism, carved a cross on them, although for generations afterwards the local people would still acknowledge the pagan gods as well, just to be on the safe side.

This coast is ideal for the traveller. It is seamed with little valleys, islands, quiet bays and beaches, and even on the

Menhir of St Duzec

Lannion

.most crowded day it is quite possible to find somewhere quiet. When the sun goes down, you can always retreat down the coast to Trébeurden or inland to Lannion.

This part of the coast, between Ploumanac'h and Trébeurden, is often referred to as the Brittany *Corniche,* and Trébeurden is particularly famous for its pink rocks, (hence the Granit-Rose coast) and for the curious shapes into which they have been eroded. Many of the rocks have acquired curious names.

Trébeurden overlooks Lannion bay with a number of islands, giving perfect sailing for small boats in the prevailing westerly winds. The side road through Pleumeur-Bodou, past the domed Space Station, leads away from the coasts of the Brittany *Corniche,* but, as elsewhere, there are plenty of byways to explore before crossing the estuary of the little Léguer and reaching Lannion.

Lannion is the southern centre for the *Corniche* and capital of Trégor, and you can turn east again here, along the valley, under the escarpment, back towards Tréguier, under the sheltering northern escarpment.

Lannion is a very old town, full of medieval sites. Brélévenez church was built by the Templars and can be viewed after a considerable climb. It has been much altered since the Templars' time and from the crypt to the tower you will ascend from the Romanesque style, then through the Gothic and arrive at the Flamboyant. From the tower there are fine views of the town and the river valley.

Lannion, a restful place after the windy, wavy coast, is a good centre for excursions. There are plenty of small comfortable hotels and at least one excellent restaurant, the Auberge de La Porte de France. They offer all manner of seafood dishes and a wide range of fixed price menus. Advance booking is recommended.

The Léguer enters Lannion from the south, and it can be followed down to the ruins of Tonquédec, the chapel at Kerfons, and the castle at Kergrist. *Ker* is a prefix encountered frequently in Brittany meaning simply 'place'. Below Kergrist is the Chapelle-les-Sept-Saints: the Seven Sleepers. It is a crypt over which a church has been built, rather than a chapel.

To the south, minor roads, always the best, lead to Belle-Isle-en-Terre, a little place, famous for its wrestlers; wrestling is a popular and ancient Breton sport. When Charles VII was still the Dauphin and glooming around in Chinon waiting for Joan of Arc, wrestlers from Belle-Isle-en-Terre were brought to entertain him.

Nearby are two interesting chapels at Locmaria and Loc-Envel, *loc* another Breton prefix, meaning a holy place. Both are in the Flamboyant Gothic style, very similar to the English Decorated, and have remarkable wooden screens, but there are many fascinating churches to visit later in Finistère.

On the road to Guingamp, the Menez-Bré is a hill, almost a thousand feet in height, topped by a chapel. The road up to the summit is very steep indeed, but the views are stupendous. The maps suggest (correctly) that Brittany is not a mountainous country, but this *seems* like one. As the countryside is continually rolling and dipping, these hills which jut up from the mass, like the Menez-Bré, seem much higher than they are.

Guingamp is a weaving centre. One story has it that the word 'gingham' is a corruption of Guingamp and this may be so, although Guingamp is more notable for food, a reputation which seems to rest on the fine cooking at the Relais du Roy. The old town, still with the relics of ramparts, is quite small and contains one of those rare Black Virgins, 'Our Lady of Good Hope', in a Gothic basilica. There is a pilgrimage to the Virgin on the first Saturday in July, and only then is Guingamp packed with people.

There are various ways back to the coast, but we go north-west again, across the high land to St Michel-en-Grève, on a wide bay, and so to the little town of Locquirec, a delightful spot with a small harbour and lots of sandy beaches. The hotels vie with each other in excellence and all give satisfaction.

Locquirec lies west of the Douron river and so, strictly speaking belongs to the next département, Finistère. It is nevertheless, a good centre for another foray south, into the hinterland of the Côtes-du-Nord, to the castle at Rosanbo which should be visited to see the gardens by Le Notre. The gorges beyond Loc-Envel are where the streams and rivers run north out of the Argoat. Here, at Lanrivain, near St Nicolas-de-Pélem, is a Breton calvary, small but with large and imposing figures, a foretaste of things to come. So west again, out at last from the comfortable Côtes-du-Nord, into a region far less familiar, the Breton heartland of Finistère, jutting out into the wild Atlantic, and quite unlike anywhere else in France.

3 Finistère: The Léonais & Montagnes d'Arée

Finistère may be conveniently (though somewhat inaccurately) divided into two regions. In the north is Léon, to the south, Cornouaille. In the opening chapter the shape of Brittany was described as a wolf's head, snapping at the Atlantic — a dog is certainly far too tame. The upper jaws of this wolf can be imagined as Léon, Cornouaille is the lower, while between lies the peninsula of Crozon. This whole region, Finistère,

is the Brittany of your imagination, the place of calvaries and pardons, of people in lace *coiffes,* and of a rocky coast beaten by the full force of the Atlantic waves.

Our introduction to this region starts, modestly enough, at the little pilgrim town of St Jean-du-Doigt, St John-of-the-Finger, north of Morlaix, where even the name encourages a visit. St Jean, like many of the villages in

Morlaix

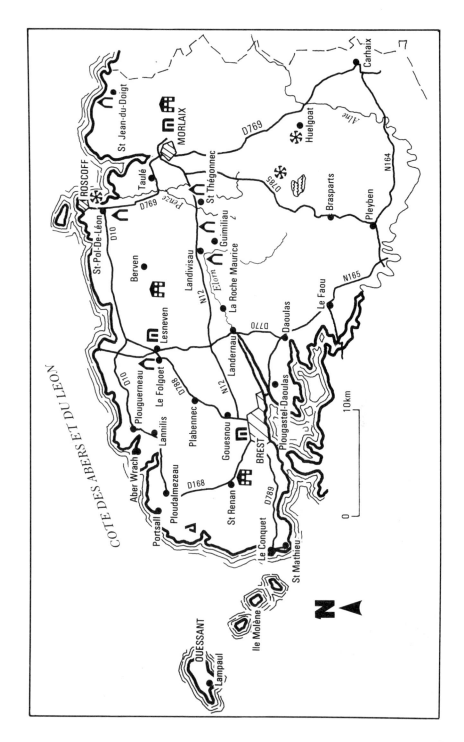

COTE DES ABERS ET DU LEON

Finistère, has a church, the size of which seems out of all proportion to the rest of the commune. The reason is that the church contains a famous relic, a finger of St John the Baptist, brought to the village in 1437, and much venerated ever since. Anne of Brittany came to pray here in 1505 and her gifts helped the local people to complete the great church.

Only the priest can give permission to see St John's reliquary, one of several in the presbytery. There is a pleasant stroll around the village to see the churchyard fountain with its carvings of St John pouring baptismal water from his cup. The architecture is modest and pleasing, the perfect gateway to Finistère.

The coast to the north of St Jean-du-Doigt is another of the typically Breton peninsulas, a maze of rocky coves and sandy beaches, peacefully secret spots on a sunny afternoon. To the west lies Morlaix bay, fed by the estuaries of the Rivers Dossen and Dourduff. Morlaix *ville* itself, some ten miles inland, is remarkable on first sight for the huge span of the massive nineteenth-century granite railway viaduct which towers two hundred feet above the streets of the town. Morlaix lies deep in the valley and was at one time a port. To a certain extent it still is, but now it is mostly yachts and small coastal vessels which find their way even so far inland. As the river really divides Finistère from Côtes-du-Nord, one bank is the Quai de Tréguier, while the other is the Quai de Léon.

World War II and time itself have not dealt too kindly with Morlaix. It has had its share of noble visitors down the years, from Mary Queen of Scots, and the ubiquitous Duchesse Anne, down to hoards of tourists in our present time. Nevertheless it remains a small market town and port, mainly interesting as a

centre for the fine surrounding countryside. There is comfortable accommodation at the Hôtel Europe or at the little motel outside the town near the autoroute, and you can eat well along the main street.

From Morlaix, those unique treasures of Brittany, the calvaries, are only a few short miles away. In the mind's eye, the calvaries of Brittany are unique. They are certainly among the sights to see, and their memory will linger long after the visit is over. They are disturbing creations, veiled, of course, in religion.

Religion means a great deal in Brittany. Even the atheist or agnostic will be unable to ignore the strong religious presence in Brittany and this does not seen to be the imposed religion of the Church Militant. The people really seem religious, and indeed, many of the pleasant things about Brittany may be rooted in the religious training and background of the people. The typical Breton is hard-working, reasonable, tidy, conscientious, friendly and family-minded.

The churches of Brittany are usually large, certainly much too large for their parishes. They are also largely late-Gothic in period and appear to be of even a later date than that. This is because they are built of granite, a stone which hardly weathers at all, and so they look much newer than they usually are. Their remarkably good condition is also due to the absence of wholehearted vandalism during the Wars of Religion and the Revolution, and to the constant care, and unrelenting toil of the parishioners. Unlike most French churches, they are full of interesting objects, paintings, carvings, tombs, statues, images and glass, while in one respect at least, they are unique.

A considerable number of Breton churches, mainly in the west and mostly in Finistère, have that peculiarly Breton addition, the *parish-close*. This usually consists of three main parts, apart from the church — a cemetary, a forest of rustic crosses, an ossuary, or charnal house, once the gathering place for old bones, and, dominating the scene, an immense and elaborately-carved calvary.

These calvaries usually consist of carvings depicting the Crucifixion, while, surrounding the crosses, will be scores, even hundreds, of figures showing scenes from the Old and New Testaments, saints and martyrs, and the odd cautionary tale. These calvaries are remarkable works of art and very often the site of spectacular local pilgrimages or pardons. The calvaries began in the late sixteenth century, during the Counter-Reformation period, or a little later, but they were inspired as much by local rivalry as religious fervour, each village vying with the next to improve and embellish its parish church and the surrounding close.

Morlaix is the ideal centre from which to visit the best of these, and the local Tourist Offices have signposted a circuit of calvaries west of Morlaix, and the first, a bare fifteen miles south-west of Morlaix, just off the road to Brest, lies at St Thégonnec. This has a large parish-close complex, complete with church, calvary, a late seventeenth-century ossuary, and a triumphal-arch. It dates from the late sixteenth century and the calvary contains scores of figures,

Calvary de St Thégonnec

47

Parish close and calvary at Lampaul-Guimiliau

Parish close, church, calvary and ossuary at Guimiliau

notably St Thégonnec and the wolves he trained to pull his plough after they had eaten his horses. There is also a portrayal of Christ at the scourging and Pilate washing his hands. The church porch, with its row of guardian saints, was once the meeting place for the Parish Council, which doubtless spent a good deal of time there wondering how to better its rival in neighbouring Guimiliau. Here is another, possibly even more magnificent, parish-close, and the calvary, apart from the usual entombment and Crucifixion, also shows the story of that unfortunate damsel, Kate Gollet, who took the devil

Musée des Jacobins
Rue des Vignes, Morlaix.
Collections of furniture, art and local
history.

The Breton Calvaries
The three finest calvaries are found
just south of Morlaix at St
Thégonnac, Guimiliau, and
Lampaul-Guimiliau.

Church of Our Lady, Le Folgöet
A very fine church on a broad green,
a famous pilgrimage church.

Duchesse Anne's House
A sixteenth-century house in the
centre of Morlaix with statues on the
façade.

Plougonven
An attractive village at the foot of the
Monts d'Arrée, with the oldest
calvary in Brittany, dating from 1554.

Ushant (Ile d'Ouessant)
This off-shore island can be reached
by boat from Brest or Le Conquet,
and the trip will take a full day. Not
advisable in bad weather.

Mill Rock and Trembling Rock,
Huelgoat
These can be found in the woods
outside Huelgoat, and are reached by
footpaths.

Roc-Tréverzel
A viewpoint in the Parc-Tréverzel.

for her lover and stole holy wafers from
the church to please him: she is being
torn to pieces by demons at one corner
of the calvary. The calvaries were often
used by the priest for his sermons, each
little scene serving to 'point a moral, or
adorn a tale'.

Lampaul-Guimiliau, a little further
on, has yet another close and a
somewhat tamer calvary, perhaps
overshadowed by the magnificent
church, but all are in the most wonderful
state of preservation. The decoration,
and above all the detail, are still intact
after almost four hundred years — a
tribute to the skill of the craftsmen and
the hardness of granite.

You can easily spend a whole day
visiting these three villages alone,
examining the details in the church and
close. This indulgence may satiate your
appetite for church architecture, at least
for a while, but at Landiviseau, you can
get a nice family lunch at the Hôtel
Floch before travelling on in the
afternoon to see the calvaries at La
Roche, La Martique, or Pécran near
Landerneau, where again you can eat
well at the Close du Pontic, before
travelling on for a brief visit to the port
and naval base at Brest.

As happened too often in Brittany
during World War II, Brest suffered
considerably as a result of Allied
bombing, French Resistance and
German tenacity. The port was, and is, a
base for the French Atlantic Fleet and
was therefore extensively used by
German U-Boats, coastal craft and large
warships. Their presence led to
continued bombing for four years by the
Allies, and the town fell only in 1944
after a prolonged siege. Although now
rebuilt in an open and agreeable
manner, little remains of the historic
seaport, which dated back to the Roman
times, and present-day Brest need not
delay us long on our travels to the West.

On the way out of Brest, however, one
catches sight of the manor of Keroual,
just before Guilers. This was once the

Ile d'Ouessant, Finistère

home of Louise de Keroual, later Duchess of Portsmouth and mistress of our own Charles II. Louise had a very adventurous career and a host of love affairs, even accompanying one lover to the wars while disguised as a cabin boy abroad his warship. She visited England in the train of Charles's aunt, the Duchess of Orleans and, after the minimum of delay, became the king's mistress. Her son by Charles, Charles Lennox, became Duke of Richmond, an English title which usually descended, whenever vacant, to some suitable

Breton connection.

West of Brest, lies the great snout of Brittany, terminating in the Pointe de St Mathieu, below le Conquet, where we turn north for the fjord-like contours of the Côte des Abers.

From anywhere along this coast almost the nearest land to the west is America. The exceptions are the maze of islands off the shore, Molène, Quémenès, Balanec, each with its belt of surf and, on the horizon, the shadowy bulk of Ouessant.

Ouessant, or as the English sailors call

Notre-Dame du Folgoet, Finistère

it, Ushant, is still the gateway to Europe for the western voyager. For centuries every sailor made his first landfall at Ushant, to check the position before bearing up for the Channel ports and home, and even today, the lighthouse at de Créach'h beams a welcome to the west. The island itself, (not large, of only some ten square miles,) enjoys a remarkably mild climate, especially in winter, unless there is a gale, in which case the waters around this coast became a maelstrom. If the weather if fair, there are excursions to the island from Brest and le Conquet, the trip taking about two hours.

Ushant is the fly hovering off the nose of the Léonais, and back on the mainland and still heading north you will soon come to the coast of the 'Abers', between Tremazan and Brignogan-Plage.

Aber, is probably not a derivative from the Welsh *aber,* which means 'river-mouth', for rivers are the one thing these deep valleys on the north coast do not have. Fjords would be a more descriptive word, for they are steep-sided valleys, probing sharply into the land.

This part of the province is called the Côte des Abers, or the 'Land of Ac'h'. For centuries it has been the home of the *göemonniers,* people who live by gathering seaweed or sea 'wrack' and piling it on the fields ashore, where, once burnt, it serves as fertilizer. These smouldering piles of weed can still be seen, although this trade, like so many ancient occupations, has declined, a fact which causes problems for the yachtsmen who frequent this coast. They find that the long seaweed, no longer intensively cropped, is quick to foul their propellers and rudders.

The Aber coast is a very beautiful part of Brittany and, like the Cornwall which it so greatly resembles, is a region full of legend. The castle of Trémazan near Portsall, for example, once sheltered Tristan and Iseult, the tragic couple from the Arthurian legend, and was certainly the birthplace of Tanguy de Châtel. He was a staunch supporter of the French Crown, who proved the fact in 1419 when he drove an axe into the head of the Duke of Burgundy at Montereau and so removed one of the king's enemies permanently from the scene. The *abers* continue north of Portsall with Aber-Benoit, and Aber-Wrac'h, both deep valleys in a rocky coast.

Apart from *abers* or estuaries, we also have *plou,* another Breton prefix meaning parish. Like the *abers,* these stand on small peninsulas, each offering peaceful, uncrowded beaches to the visitor.

Past the little yachting centre of Aber Wrac'h is Plouguerneau (quite small but with one memorable restaurant, Les Voyageurs) and then Brignogan, once, like Plouguerneau, the haunt of wreckers.

All through this country you will see numerous megaliths, or standing stones. There are supposed to be more here than in any other part of France, mostly in the form of dolmens, that is, two or three stone uprights crowned with a flat boulder, many formerly being burial chambers, and once covered with earth. They are not so plentiful as the upright menhirs at Carnac, although there is one great menhir, the 'Men-Marz', now Christianized. They are one of the sights of the region.

Le Folgoët, in the very centre of the Léonais, is a surprise. Having seen the churches at St Thégonnec and Guimiliau, we should be getting accustomed to fine churches, but those of the parish-closes are rather cramped.

Le Folgoët, on the other hand, is spread out across a wide village green, as peaceful as any village green can be.

Le Folgoët became a pilgrim centre because in the fourteenth century a simple-minded shepherd lad, called Solomon, lived there. He could speak only a few words, endlessly repeating 'Oh Lady Virgin Mary', like a mantra. After his death in 1358, a white lily sprang from his grave; on being investigated, it was found to come from Solomon's mouth, evidence of sainthood and the origin of the legend.

After the Battle of Auray in 1364, the victor, Jean de Montfort, laid the first stones of the church which is now the pilgrim centre of Notre-Dame-de-Folgoët. The church was completed in 1423 and is another place which no visitor to Brittany should miss. Built in the most exquisite style of the late Gothic, in hard-wearing Kersanton blue granite, its architecture, both inside and out, is quite magnificent.

Le Folgoët was famous enough to attract the Duchesse Anne in 1505 and the mob in 1793, but the local stones stood up well to their rustic battering, and most of the statuary and bracing still survives. The interior of the church is striking and the hall opposite, with the cardinals' arms in the porch (now a museum) is a Renaissance jewel.

Le Folgoët lies in the centre of the Léonais and you can return towards Morlaix through Kerjean and Lambader for further forays. The castle at Kerjean now belongs to the State and very stately it is. It has been referred to as the 'Versailles of Brittany', but that, on size alone, is greatly overstating the case, while in no way diminishing Kerjean's other attractions.

It stands at the end of a long tree-lined drive and is protected by a moat. Moats were a trifle unnecessary for the period in which Kerjean was built, between 1560 and 1590, but Brittany had many other moated castles, which is no doubt why the builder, Louis Barbier, provided one here. It is a Renaissance manor, built on a central square. The entrance is across a drawbridge and through an arch, where on one side is the pigeon-loft and on the other the pillars of the gallows from which the Lord of Kerjean exercised his role as magistrate and hanged the local malefactors. A few guards and a hangman were very necessary residents in the hall of the sixteenth-century French noble, although, (such are the twists if history) the last owners of Kerjean were themselves guillotined in 1794.

Berven, to the north, has another calvary, but of no great merit, and you can press on past Lambader, which has a fine late-Gothic church, and so back to Morlaix.

Morlaix is a market centre for the Northern Léonais, but hardly the place to stay. Hotels in Brittany, especially on the coast, are plentiful but in fact Morlaix has very few and only one, the Europe in the centre, of any merit.

To the north, staying close to the 'ria', or estuary of the Penze, are two interesting towns, St Pol-de-Léon, with its remarkable church, and the Channel ferry-port of Roscoff.

St Pol was the seat of the first bishopric in Brittany and takes its name from St Paul, or St Pol, the Aurelian; a cathedral only remains a cathedral while it contains the seat of a bishop, and the Bishopric of St Pol has long since disappeared. The church of St Pol, not large but very well-proportioned, is now overshadowed by the nearby fourteenth-century chapel of the Krisker, where the belfry, itself inspired by the Norman spires at Caen, was in turn the model for most of the towers and pinnacles in

Château de Kerjean

Brittany.

Roscoff has a church, an interesting aquarium, medieval walls, some nice houses and gardens in the old *bourg* and a fine port which ships out all the local produce and, most notably, the artichoke, the 'almost-emblem' of Breton agriculture. The whole region around St Pol and Roscoff is a market garden area, and all the vegetables are superb.

Roscoff was, and to an extent still is, the departure point for the Breton onion-sellers who were once a regular sight on the roads of England, pedalling along on their onion-festooned bicycles, and appearing at the back door for a chat and a rapid sale.

Off Roscoff, a mere ten minutes by boat, lies the little isle of Batz, while from the town itself you can look south across the bay to the spires of St Pol, and the little town of Carentec, another seaside resort of considerable charm, on yet another peninsula.

The sea dominates Brittany. It seems to be always there. Since the Breton shores are attractive, this is no great hardship, but we now go inland, away from the sea, as far as that is possible in Brittany, to the Argoat and the Montagnes d'Arrée.

Armorica, you will recall, means 'the land facing the sea'. The Argoat, on the other hand, 'the country of wood', and refers to the hinterland of the region. Once upon a time this might have been very true, but today much of the great Breton forest land has gone. Nevertheless, Brittany is still a very wooded country, and if there are few great forests, there is no lack of woodland and great oak trees.

South of Morlaix lies Huelgoat, capital of the Argoat, and to the east the Montagnes d'Arrée and the gateway to the Parc Regional d'Armorique. A

55

glance at a topographic map reveals just how rumpled this countryside is, and although the 'mountains' are not high, and really not mountains at all, they are rolling and rugged. The Parc Regional d'Armorique covers most of the Montagnes d'Arrée, and begins in the west at le Faou, running east and a little north towards Huelgoat. Trévezel Rock, north-west of Huelgoat, at 384 metres (1,248ft) is the ideal place from which to view the mountains to the south and the sea-coast to the rear.

Huelgoat is the centre of great walking country. From the river Argent in the middle of the town, marked walks and *Grande Randonnée* trails lead off in all directions, along steep paths.

Although not really high, with all the hills here being less than 700ft, it certainly seems hilly. Not far from the centre lies the *roche tremblante,* the rocking stone, which, although weighing over two tons, will sway if you put your shoulder to it.

All the *sentiers* have names, and it would take a week to walk them all. The woods are beautiful in autumn, full of rushing brooks with little waterfalls, and the town is full of good hotels, very popular all the year round with hikers and fishermen. One good excursion is to walk through the woods for lunch at the little routier cafe, the Amis des Routiers on the road south to Carhaix.

The main mass of the Montagnes

Detail of Calvary at Brasparts

d'Arrée lies to the west of Huelgoat and a series of little roads leads into it. Only the most minor roads lead to such out-of-the-way places. The Arrée countryside is very varied with its open moors and forests, and the St Michel reservoir provides a huge lake in the centre near Brasparts, where, inevitably, the local people keep their boats.

Brasparts itself lies below the height of St Michel de Brasparts. There is a chapel on the top of this mount, or *menez,* from which is a fine view across the countryside, north-west to the peninsula of Plougastel-Daoulas, famous for strawberries, while shipping can be seen in the Brest roads. Directly west lies another height of Ren-ar-Hoat-ar-Gosse, very Breton, skirted by the D42 before running down to le Faou.

The little town of le Faou is remarkably pretty when the tide is in, but at full ebb, it stands alone in a wilderness of mudflats and marshes. As the tide comes in le Faou turns back into the pretty place of its reputation.

Le Faou stands at the very tip of the Brest roads, a vast and perfect anchorage, which leads through the Goulet channel out to the Atlantic, and was once itself a medieval port.

The road leads a little way north-west to Daoulas and on to another great calvary at Plougastel-Daoulus (where Kate Gollet again appears with her tormentors). From here you can go for a little tour of that peninsula, or *presqu'ile* or 'almost-an-island', before returning to le Faou to prepare for the next stage south into the land of Cornouaille.

4 Southern Finistère: Châteaulin to Quimperle

The Ménez-Hom, at the base of the Presqu'ile de Crozon, is a windy moorland hill, a thousand feet above the sea, dominating the neck of the peninsula, and a little way south of Le Faou.

To reach it from Le Faou one drives along the Aulne estuary past some moored warships of the Reserve Fleet, swinging on their rusty anchor chains, and over the Aulne bridge at Térénez. The sparking Aulne is an interesting river, not only here on the beautiful wooded estuary but also further inland, around Châteaulin. It contains salmon and sea-trout and one can almost walk across it dry-shod, on the decks of moored craft. Once across and past the calvary at Argol, there is a choice of routes and you can take both in turn, but first drive on, into Ste-Marie-du-Ménez-Hom, park by the church and walk across the moor and bracken up to the Ménez-Hom itself. From the crest there are immense views in every direction, but your gaze will be directed naturally to the west, over the Presqu'ile.

The huge bay to the south is the Bay of Douarnenez and, at the neck of the Cap de la Chèvre which juts south, lies the resort of Morgat, not surprisingly, a sailing centre, wonderfully sheltered

Bay of Douarnenez

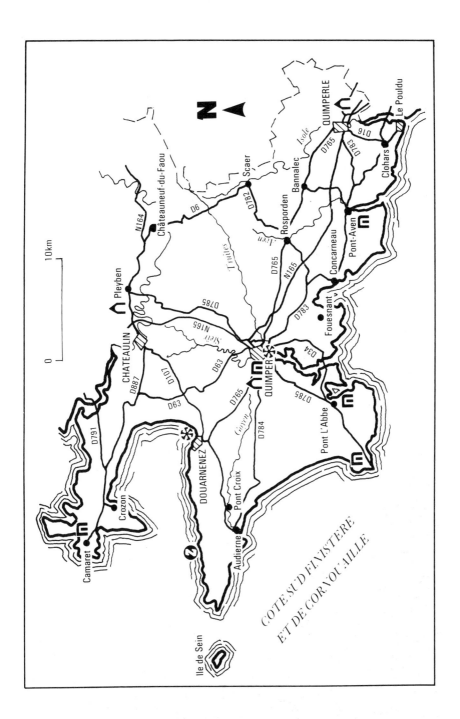

COTE SUD FINISTERE
ET DE CORNOUAILLE

within the great bay and with excellent walks across the crest of the peninsula to the rival resort of Camaret on the Toulinquet reach. Camaret, more exposed to rough seas than Morgat, has several off-setting advantages. Those who are great lovers of shellfish should make directly for Camaret, the premier lobster port of France. There are a number of good restaurants around the *quai,* usually full of Frenchmen, eating with great gusto.

Those of a more intellectual turn of mind will be interested in the pilgrim chapel of Rocamadour, or in visiting the Naval Museum in Camaret. It was off Camaret in 1801 that the American inventor Robert Fulton, put his prototype submarine to its first test. His craft was small and leaky and could only just submerge, but a British frigate blockading Brest came conveniently into the bay and Fulton and his crew duly gurgled below and set off to sink here. Fulton's submersible was propelled by oars and after floundering around below the surface of the bay for some hours, they surfaced, gasping, to discover that the frigate had hauled her sheets and sailed away. However, Fulton set an example. The German U-boat fleet sailed from this coast during World War II and wrought more destruction on the British than that early pioneer could ever have imagined.

The Crozon peninsula is divided at the top into three smaller outcrops: Roscanvel, Penhir and Cap de la Chèvre. Each contains little bays, quite deserted even in the busiest months, and this region is well worth exploring.

The Bay of Douarnenez can be reached along the coast, or via Châteaulin on the Aulne, a great fishing

Crozon, Finistère

Calvary at Pleyben

centre. This would be my chosen route, for after lunch on local trout or salmon at the Auberge Ducs-de-Lin you can press on inland to Pleyben.

The church and calvary at Pleyben are quite outstanding and the setting for both, amid tall trees, is quite magnificent. The church is part-Gothic and part-late-sixteenth-century, all blending wonderfully well, while the figures in the calvary are extremely delicate. Although carved in the late-sixteenth century, they are dressed in the mid-fifteenth-century style and seem for that reason more credible. The interior of the church is in the light and airy style of the early Baroque, with fine statues and a blue star-spangled barrel vault.

After Pleyben — and you may have to drag yourself away — the valley of the Aulne leads to Châteauneuf-du-Faou, where the river is really beautiful. Locronon, to the south-west, is a fine granite town, quiet and peaceful except once in every seven years when, on the second Sunday in July, a week-long religious festival begins, (although a smaller, one-day affair — La Trömenie Pardon — is held every year).

At Douarnenez, towards the coast, one can enjoy another excellent meal and look out on the pleasing vista of the seaport from the Restaurant Les Mouettes, on the Plage du Ris. Try the *jambon au Madère* with a bottle of chilled Muscadet — delicious!

Douarnenez, though a holiday centre, is first and foremost a commercial fishing port. You will need to skirt the commercial port before you arrive at the *quais,* where the fishing boats are tied up in rows. Painted in all colours, reds, greens, ambers and yellows, they glow on the water in the evening sun. Further on towards Audierne, you will pass beside a creek where the hulls and hulks of old boats are rotting away on the mud, for here, as elsewhere, the fishing has declined.

A minor road outside Douarnenez leads west, along the north shore of the Sizun peninsula. This is by far the best way to reach the Pointe du Raz, being less *touristique,* and half way along on the right, lies the nature reserve of Cap Sizun. Seabirds are a feature of Brittany and are nowhere seen to better advantage than at Sizun. (You will need good fieldglasses and a head for heights.) Birdwatchers are admitted to the Reserve only in small parties, but the birds can be seen in great numbers and variety. Gulls galore, of course, but also auks, kittiwakes, cormorants, puffins on the grassy slopes, as well as ravens and choughs on the steep cliffs along the shore.

This northern route is much less developed than the southern and comes out on the Pointe du Raz, overlooking the beautiful, but sinister, Baie des Trépassés, the 'Bay of the Dead'. Onshore currents bring the bodies of drowned sailors here, from craft wrecked on the reefs on the Pointe du Raz, a discovery which makes the blue waters seem suddenly uninviting.

Under the waters of the Bay of the Dead lies the legendary city of Y's. Whether Y's ever existed is debatable. It is as legendary as Lyonesse but, so the legend goes, it was the capital of Cornouaille, and the home of a King Gradlon whose daughter, Duhat, fell in love with the Devil. The Devil asked her to open the sluices which kept the seas from the town and as the waters drowned the city, he deserted her. She fled for safety with her father, but the waves were overtaking them when a heavenly voice directed the king to cast his daughter into the waves. The king obeyed, losing his daughter and his city to the seas off Trépassés.

We shall mention King Gradlon again at Quimper, where he retreated after the flood. The bay, then, is not just a beautiful place, but like so many other places in Brittany, a place of legend and superstition, where the sea beats in from the west and cares very little for anyone who gets in the way. For all that, the bay is very attractive, and you sweep down and up to the lighthouse and cliffs of the Pointe du Raz, the most westerly point

Point du Raz

on the mainland of Europe, looking out over the Raz de Sein and the Ile de Sein itself.

This is a dangerous, villainous coast, frightening in a westerly gale, when the waters become a maelstrom of huge waves and hurtling spray. People come out here to view the storms in winter as well as the blue seas in summer, and their constant feet have worn the grass off the Pointe, exposing the bare rock and making it a bleak, if beautiful, place, in spite of the tourist shops.

The Ile de Sein, which can be visited from Audierne, is an interesting place, mainly because of its inhabitants. They may appear no different from other Breton people, but they have unusual qualities. The men are fishermen, and all the work ashore, even in the small fields and gardens, is women's work; the men will not touch it. In former times, the men made a better living by wrecking, luring ships on to the rocks where they could be pillaged, another activity shared, once upon a time, by their kinfolk in Cornwall.

However, in the last war, the men of

Bay of Trépassés

---

the Sein showed sterner qualities. After a public meeting, the *entire* male population of the island sailed for England in June 1940, and enlisted with the Free French Army. This included a thirteen-year-old boy who was most annoyed at being sent off to school immediately on arrival. General de Gaulle remarked, at his first review, how strange it was that 'little Sein had provided me with a quarter of the soldiers of France.'

Once home again, and proudly displaying their Medal of the Liberation which de Gaulle awarded to the island, the men soon discovered a new industry. From the days of the *Ancien Regime,* the inhabitants of Sein had been exempt from such taxation as the *gabelle,* or salt tax. When income tax was universally introduced in France, they were excluded from this also, since the

revenue from such a bleak and barren spot would hardly be worth collecting. However, in 1949 the French Government was somewhat disturbed to discover that the islanders were offering their home to industry as a tax haven! An Act was rushed through parliament introducing taxation there, to stop the practice, at which the islanders promptly went on a tax strike. The end of it all was effectively to discourage big business, while leaving the islanders still enjoying their immemorial rights.

Audierne, on the south shore of Cap Sizun, is another fishing port, and a great centre for *langoustines,* best eaten locally at the little restaurant Le Goyen (named after the local river) in the Place Jean-Simon. Here, apart from the delicious seafood, the food is well served with vegetables grown on the local hills; Audierne, like Roscoff, is a market

Veryach

Coastal fishing

Pornichet

La Baule

PLACES OF INTEREST NEAR DOURNENEZ

Fish Auction, Rosmeur Harbour, Dournenez
These take place every morning, and the jetty gives good views over fishing boats and harbour.

Pointe du Raz
At the end of the Sizun peninsula, 36km (22 miles) west of Dournenez, with a wild seascape out to the Ile de Sein.

Ménez-Hom
The tallest hill hereabouts, at the head of the Presqu'ile de Crozon, with fine views over the coast.

Bird Reserve, Cap Sizun
A seabird sanctuary 21km (12 miles) west of Dournenez. Open: Easter-October. Guided visits possible.

Musée Bigouden, Pont L'Abbé
A collection of local furniture and *coiffes.*

L'eglise, Pont l'Abbé

centre. St Tugen, nearby, built after 1500, is a place of pilgrimage, where the saint is said to provide an effective safeguard against rabies. His 'pardon' on 24 June is always well supported for this reason.

To the south of Audierne, across another immense bay, the Bay of Audierne, is the lonely calvary at Tronöen, and the Pointe de Penmarc'h. Unlike most calvaries which stand in villages, that at Tronöen is in the country. As this is the oldest calvary in Brittany, perhaps this one follows the original intention, to be built in lonely places, away from the haunts of men. After all, the first one was 'without a city wall' and this one at Tronöen is certainly the most moving of them all, and in view of its age is in remarkably good condition.

The rocks at Guénolé are another trap for ships, but the Museum of Prehistory there is worth visiting before pressing on into Morbihan, the most famous region of Brittany, to see the menhirs and megaliths.

From here, at Penmarc'h, we turn north, to Pont l'Abbé and enter the so-called 'Bigouden' district, home of the most familiar of all the Breton *coiffes*, a tall, white pillar worn high on the top of the head. How it stays in place in all winds and weathers is a mystery, but the women (and alas, only old women seem to wear it now) manage very well. (I saw one woman, head erect, indifferent to the winds of the Pointe de Raz, while we were met at Pont l'Abbé by a woman in a tall *coiffe* pedalling madly downhill on a bicycle, again without loss of her crowning glory.)

Pont l'Abbé is the centre of the *pays bigouden,* the part of Brittany which has

Woodcarving in Locronan

Pont L'Abbé

best retained its old traditions, and worth a visit for the certainty of seeing one of the Breton *coiffes*. It is also a good centre for exploring the Bigouden country itself, up to the capital of Cornouaille at Quimper.

We now travel east, for we are on the southern coast of Brittany, and proceed across the new toll bridge over the Odet into Benodet. This can be recommended as *the* place to stay when visiting the Bigouden coast. It has fine clear waters with good sailing, very popular with the British, and yachtsmen of all nations. It also has a delightful wooded hinterland, while offshore lie the Glenan Islands, home of a famous sailing school and a great sanctuary for seabirds, which can

be visited from Benodet or Concarneau.

Quimper, on the River Odet, is very clearly a capital city. Although quite small, with only 60,000 people, it is dominated by the huge Gothic facade of St Corentin's cathedral, built between the twelfth and fifteenth century and almost entirely completed within the Gothic period. The two spires which top the towers were added only in the last century, but they are extremely fine, and blend in exactly with the original building. The mounted figure between the two towers is King Gradlon, King of the City of Y's.

Gradlon retired to Quimper after his kingdom disappeared, and was consoled by St Corentin. Until the Revolution, the

Bénodet, Finistère

townsfolk used to send the king a drink, one a year, on St Cecilia's Day. The man who climbed the tower would offer the drink to the king — which was naturally refused — drink it himself, and throw the glass into the crowd below. Anyone catching it unbroken, which must have been a fairly hazardous task, earned a handsome prize provided by the Town Council, who would go to considerable lengths, such as filing through the glass-stem, to ensure that unbroken catches were very rare events.

Opposite the cathedral lies the old town, well worth a visit, especially to wander along the Rue Kéréon, with its old houses and fine shops. There is a range of good restaurants along the Avenue de la Gare, and a comfortable night available at the Hôtel La Tour d'Auvergne, named after the Breton soldier who fought with surpassing gallantry in the Napoleonic wars. The hotel is decorated with frescoes depicting his exploits, that outside the dining room is particularly apt, showing the gallant grenadier storming a Prussian camp crying *Qui veut diner, me suit!* ('Anyone who wants to dine, follow me!'). He clearly knew how to inspire French soldiers to the charge.

The Brittany Museum near the cathedral should be seen by all visitors to Quimper. It offers a complete record of Breton history, and, most unusually in a museum, offers folklore as well as factually-correct historical exhibits. So much of Brittany's history is based on legends that any account which leaves them out, while possibly more accurate, remains sterile. On the opposite side of the cathedral is the Musée des Beaux Arts, which has a fine collection of paintings, including some by Fragonard and Corot, and this will make a useful introduction to the artistic milieu we shall shortly visit Pont-Aven. For a tour of the Odet estuary you can take a boat from Quimper down to Benodet itself.

For Pont-Aven go south to Fouesnant, where the Hôtel Armorique has an unsurpassed table and across the bay a fine view of the next major stop, the fishing port and walled town of Concarneau.

This is another fishing port. Brittany lives from the sea, and on the face of it, when you have said *that* you have said, if not everything, then a very great deal. On the other hand, their ports are all different and Concarneau is one of the most unusual.

It began and developed on the island in the centre of the harbour, now occupied by the *ville close*. A walk around the walls of the *ville close,* surrounded by the colourful moored fishing fleet, is the highlight of a visit. On the third Sunday in August the port is at its best during the *Bleu Filet* fête, when the blue nets of the port's fishermen are hung everywhere among a host of bunting and the gay costumes of the fisherfolk. Concarneau, naturally enough is full of good restaurants and the food is especially good at La Belle Etoile, on the Cabellou-Plage.

East of Concarneau lies Pont-Aven, not in itself remarkable, but an agreeable resort. It was once the centre for Paul Gauguin and his friends who developed the artistic style which has since become famous as the Pont-Aven school. Gauguin moved to Pont-Aven from Paris in 1886, and soon began to attract a group of followers. By 1888, after a short visit to Panama by Gauguin, they had become a self-supporting community, and Gauguin began, with another painter, Emile Bernard, to develop a unique style of painting, going far beyond the Impressionist style. The established

Cathedral porch, Quimper

Quimper Cathedral

painters painted what was *there*, the
Impressionists painted what they *saw*,
which is by no means the same thing,
while Gauguin believed in painting what
he *felt*.

There is a story of Gauguin finding
one of his friends, Serusier, painting in
the woods near Pont-Aven. 'How do
you see that tree?' he asked him. 'You
say yellow, very well. That shadow is
blue — let it be pure ultramarine, and as
for these red leaves, they seem to me to
be vermilion.' Gauguin and Bernard
called this style *Cloisonnism*
(partitioning), and the effects were quite
startling. In Gauguin's case, the violent
colour contrasts were enhanced by
jagged shapes, sharp outlines and flat
layers of colour, a complete departure
from the Impressionist ideal.

In 1890 Gauguin and Bernard
exhibited their work, which had been
barred from the official display, in a café
next to the central hall of the Paris
Exhibition. Their exhibition presented a
hundred paintings, and none was sold,
but certain critics did at least begin to
grasp what the Pont-Aven school was
trying to say: 'that in art it is more
creative to interpret than to copy'.

Pont-Aven still attracts artists today.
The River Aven, which pours through
the town, no longer drives the mills it
powered a hundred years ago, but much
of the town remains as it was in
Gauguin's day. The Moulin de
Rosmadec still stands, and the food is
excellent, while in the centre, the Hôtel
d'Ajoncs, recalls another of Gauguin's
friends, Theodore Botrel, a poet, who
lived in Pont-Aven, and started an arts
festival, the *Fête des Fleurs d'Ajoncs,* the
'gorse flower festival', still held here in
early August. From the centre you can
walk up the valley, through the Bois
d'Amour to the chapel at Tremelo,
where Gauguin painted his 'Yellow
Christ', and back along the river bank, a
walk made a thousand times by the
paint-spattered artists of the Pont-Aven
school.

If you go east again, you will cross
several estuaries, for this south coast has
more large rivers than that of the north,
until you come to the banks of the Laita,
where you turn north for Quimperlé.
This road will take you into the forest of
Carnoët, pleasant enough now, but one
with a grisly tale to tell, another of the
Breton legends mentioned earlier, quite
unlikely and yet frequently believed.

Here, long ago, lived the County of
Carnoët, who heard from a fortune-
teller that his first-born son would kill
him and inherit his lands. He therefore
murdered his wives as soon as they

became pregant! His fifth wife managed to flee before the news broke, and eventually bore a son, who became St Trémeur. Eventually the count met the saint and, recognising him instantly as his son, chopped off his head! The saint, quite undaunted, picked up his head and followed the count back to his castle. There he threw a handful of earth against the walls, at which the entire place collapsed on top of the wicked baron. Exactly *how* St Trémeur became a saint is not revealed, but he is shown in statue carrying his head around, as, apparently, saints were able to do at will. As Brittany is supposed to have over 7,000 saints, it must have been difficult to be different.

There is also the story of a priest who told a very sceptical lady the story of St Denis, who, although beheaded on Montmartre, was able to carry his head ten miles to his church of St Denis outside the city. 'Ten miles, madame' said the priest. 'Now that was a miracle.' 'One step would have been a miracle', replied the lady tartly. But the point of a legend is not that it is true, but that it is believed!

Quimperlé, on the very border of Finistère, hard against Morbihan, is in the valley of the Lafta, a river formed by the joining of two smaller streams, the Isole and the Elle, which join here. The town centre is over-shadowed by a massive church, St Michael's, and filled by the bulk of another church, St Croix.

St Croix was first built in the early twelfth century in the style of the Holy Sepulchre in Jerusalem, probably from drawings brought home by the victorious survivors of the First Crusade. Solid as it now appears, the church collapsed in the last century, and had to be rebuilt, fortunately in the same style, although the rebuilt belfry, the cause of the original collapse, now stands apart from the main church.

Quimperlé has some nice old houses, notably in the Rue Dom-Morice, a very short street, where, it was reputed, the houses leaned so far towards each other that the inhabitants could shake hands from the upstairs windows — not true of course, unless they had very long arms, but an attractive street for all that.

In the Rue Bremond d'Ars, is the garden of the now ruined church of St Colomban. On its wall is the effigy of a twelfth-century knight, still in excellent condition, with a broad sword and touches of the original paint and gilding, and for all the other charms of this attractive town this little garden is my favourite spot in Quimperlé.

Finistère is the most unusual and least French of all the Breton *départements*. A lifetime could be spent exploring its thousand little valleys and coves and hidden places, and any time to spare could not be better spent, but it is time to go north again, to le Faouët, and the land of *Mor-bi-han,* the land of the little sea.

5 The Western Morbihan: Le Faouet to Lorient

The northern road from Quimperlé runs quickly into woods. In autumn the wind blows the yellow leaves off the trees in a golden snowstorm, covering the roads in a thick, colourful carpet.

The Roche au Diable, off the road to le Faouët and overlooking the river, is a jumble of huge rocks and narrow footpaths. The view from the rocks, down to the river, is obscured by the trees, so only a brief stop is needed before pressing on, past St-Fiacre to le Faouët.

Le Faouët is the centre for visiting the Montagnes Noires, a range of wooded hills running across the centre of Finistère into Morbihan. They are fairly well forested and, like most Breton mountains, are not particularly high, although it is good walking country. Le Faouët itself is a pleasant place, remarkable only for a huge market hall, dating from the mid-1500s. Inside is a fantastic network of beams and rafters.

East of le Faouët, past the chapel of St Nicolas, lies Kernascléden. There is a

Market Hall, Le Faouët

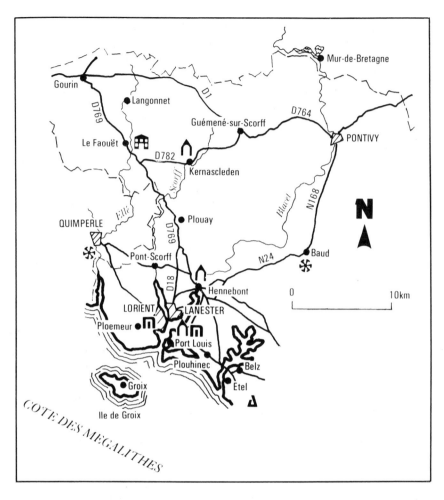

wide choice of little chapels in this area, and all are worth visiting, especially on foot along the *sentiers,* but to be selective, choose that at Kernascléden, acclaimed as a masterpiece of the Breton Gothic style. It was built in 1453, the year in which the English were finally expelled from France, with rare skill and attention to detail. Breton churches tend to feature six apostles in the porch, but Kernascléden has two porches and, therefore, includes all twelve. The interior is a riot of stone and frescoes, and there is another 'Doom' which

illustrates in gruesome detail the tortures which await the Damned after they arrive in Hell.

From Kernascléden minor roads lead north and east to Pontivy on the river Blavet. A topographic map shows that the Blavet runs down a valley from the forest of Quénécan, out to the sea at Lorient and skirts the hills of Landes de Lanvaux.

From Pontivy, where you can stay comfortably at the Hôtel Porhöet, you can tour north to the little village of Mur-de-Bretagne and around the great lake at Guerlédan.

The Canal-de-Nantes-Brest runs through here; deserted now, its towpath is still intact and provides a good walking route through the *Argoat.* Some parts of this area are carved into deep rocky gorges, like those of Poulancre nearby, and these have quite different scenery from the surrounding countryside, which is largely devoted to mixed agriculture, forestry and quarries.

Pontivy has an old *bourg* with the remains of a moated medieval château-fort, and a new town, built during the First Empire and known for a time as Napoleonville, partly to emphasise the town's loyalty to the emperor, partly to celebrate the opening of the canal, which was constructed on the emperor's orders to divert his coastal shipping away from the British Navy. Pontivy is the chief market town of central Brittany and south from here the Blavet, a winding, little-known river, leads to a number of interesting spots on the way.

The Blavet has been much exploited by minor industry, such as saw-mills, but of the local sort, without any satanic smoke stacks, and the river water is still pure enough for good fishing and so well-fringed with *pêcheurs.*

St Nicodème and St Nicholas-des-Eaux are two little villages on the river, both with interesting chapels. You can get a good view of the river before you come down to Baud and visit the Vénus of Quinipily.

Baud itself, minute and quickly visited, is best seen on market days or Sundays when the older women wear their *coiffes.* You can then go out on the N24 and turn off to see the Venus on her little hill.

She stands in a farmyard, overlooking the empty basin of a large, bath-tub-like fountain. The stone statue is bigger than life-size, and so resembles the lid of a mummy's tomb that its Eastern and pagan origins are immediately obvious.

The origins of the figure are unknown, but she has an Egyptian aspect, is certainly over 2,000 years old, and far from beautiful. One theory maintains that she was brought from Egypt by one of the occupying legions in about 56BC, and she was certainly in Brittany when the first Christian missionaries arrived in about AD250, for they took violent exception to such a pagan image and the Venus was promptly hurled into a nearby river. This happened frequently down the centuries without avail, for she was always secretly retrieved and replaced by the local people. The priests then hurled her back into the river and again she was recovered. She was eventually hidden in a cave and remained there until she was placed over the fountain in 1695. Somewhat worn out by all this excitement, she had to be taken down and recarved in the late 1700s, and restored to the present position where she now stands, through all weather, greeting the visitor with an enigmatic and rather weary gaze, which, after all she had endured, is hardly surprising.

Hennebont is a surprise. It starts as a straggling village, a typical *village-rue,* and apparently without interest until you reach the main square, the Place Maréchal-Foch, and are at once delighted. Hennebont must join the list of places in Brittany which every traveller should see. It also contains the Château de Locguénolé, a fine hotel and restaurant on the banks of the river where the food is excellent. Opposite the cathedral is the Hôtel de la Poste which is much cheaper, serves good food and attracts crowds of local people for lunch on Sunday. The Place Foch is dominated by the great church of Our Lady of Paradise, which really is huge

Medieval gateway, Hennebont

and, in a small town, quite overwhelming.

The traveller in Brittany will be struck by the number of churches dedicated to Our Lady. Most of the Breton churches were built in the twelfth and thirteenth centuries when the idea of chivalry was taking root in Western Christendom, and, among other things, this meant a rise in the status of women. Previously, women had been little more than chattels, useful for their dowry and to breed sons. Chivalry became symbolized by the ideas of courtly love and this led to the cult of the Virgin. Previously, churches had been dedicated to a local saint and were frequently erected on a former pagan site and consecrated by the early Church. Most of the Breton churches we see today, however, are survivals from the Late Gothic period and are often built in the Flamboyant or

Decorated style. Romanesque churches were very rare, having been destroyed by the Northmen, and as most churches in Brittany were built in enduring granite, churches in a later period were largely superfluous. Indeed, Breton churches are almost always too large for any possible modern congregation.

Our Lady of Paradise was built well after the town, in the years between 1513 and 1530. The town itself is of much earlier date and was walled by 1237.

The last war destroyed much of Hennebont and only remnants of the old walls remain, but you can climb up on them and walk down to the Blavet, looking down into the gardens, and the streets of the town. The river is still capable of taking coastal craft and the town was once a port. In 1345 an English fleet sailed up the river to lift the siege of the town, then under attack by

PLACES TO VISIT IN THE WESTERN
MORBIHAN

Carnöet Forest
This begins 4km (2 miles) south of
Quimperlé, good for walks or car
tours.

The Venus of Quimpily
Just outside Baud, on the road to
Hennebont, a very old statue over a
fountain.

Atlantic Museum
The Citadel, Port Louis
Large museum to the World War II
Battle of the Atlantic.

Larmor
An attractive seaside resort close to
Lorient. The medieval church
includes a rare Jew's altar, and on the
Sunday closest to 24 June, there is a
blessing of the sea.

Boat Trips
To Belle Isle from Port Louis, Port
Tudy or Lorient.

St Cado
A small island, between Lorient and
Auray, with an interesting chapel
across a causeway.

the French. The English held Hennebont
for twenty-seven years before it fell
eventually, and inevitably, to
Duguesclin.

Hennebont was once a port, but
Lorient on the Blavet estuary, has been
one of the great Naval arsenals of
France since the seventeenth century. As
it suffered considerably in the last war,
for a better view, and to start a visit,
travel down the left bank of the river to
the Vauban fortress of Port Louis.

The French, too, had an East India
Company, as indeed did the Dutch. The
Compagnie des Indes was financed by the
king and private speculators; Louis XIII
and Richelieu originally established the
company at Port Louis, but Colbert
later moved it into Le Havre. Here the
English took such a toll of the laden
Indiamen as they made their way home
up the Channel that Louis XIV and his
Chief Minister, Mazerin, re-established
the company at the specially built port
of Lorient, or L'Orient, and the *des
Indes* became the more resonant-
sounding *Compagnie de L'Orient.*

The port of Lorient, which lies inside
the estuary, was protected by the fortress
town of Port Louis on the point. This
was also built by Richelieu, and named
after Louis XIII, although it was
originally called Blavet. Port Louis
today is a tribute to the military genius
of Vauban and a perfect example of
seventeenth-century military
fortification. The citadel of the port,
reached across a sea-moat by a narrow
drawbridge, now contains a naval
museum. The neighbouring *fosse*
contains a memorial to resistance
fighters shot here for spying on the
movements of U-boats operating from
the German submarine-pens, which can
still be seen across the estuary, in
Lorient.

The German submarine fleet ravaged
British shipping in the Atlantic from the
first days of World War II, when a U-
boat sank the liner *Athenia* with a great
loss of life. The submarine menace really
expanded with the fall of France in June
1940, when the German Navy obtained
possession of the Breton ports of Brest,
Lorient and St Nazaire, and thereby
gained much extra range. Any details of
submarine activity were vital to Allied
Naval Intelligence and the local French
Resistance took great risks to obtain

Port Louis

them, frequently, as here, with fatal results to themselves. Allied air raids on the submarine bases led to the construction of bomb-proof submarine pens, some of which can still be seen from the walls of Port Louis. The pens were persistently bombed, but this did more damage to the surrounding townships than to the U-boats within, and, in the course of the raids, the centres of many of these old towns were completely destroyed. Not until 1944 were there bombs of sufficient size and power to penetrate the reinforced concrete of the pens, and in most cases, they still remain, as a memorial to a savage period in sea warfare, and in some cases, as workshops for the present French Navy.

Turning away from these grisly reminders of the past and after a morning basking — tide permitting — on the wide sandy beach below the walls of the citadel at Port Louis, one can lunch at the Hôtel Avel Vor, opposite the port, and turn one's attention to Breton food.

Brittany is not one of the great gastronomic regions of France, and its main claim to culinary fame rests on the variety and excellence of the sea food. A devoted meat-eater would be disappointed in Brittany. This said, to those who like sea food and are not great gourmets, but nevertheless enjoy good food, Brittany has a great deal to offer.

To begin with, food in Brittany is well-cooked, carefully served, plentiful in portions, and relatively inexpensive. The over-all standard of cooking is consistently high and bad meals are very rare. Bearing in mind the Breton generosity, caution is needed when ordering a meal, for the portions served can be shattering. (A 'starter' of *langoustine,* when counted, contained twenty-three of these giant cray-fish! A plate of *moules-farcies,* again when counted, contained eighteen succulent mussels!)

Prices are always rising and in a guide book which will stay in print for some time, one must be wary of quoting prices too specifically. However, the standard four to five course menu currently costs from about F45 (about £4 at the current rate of exchange). One such meal a day is as much as most travellers need, and this again is usually reserved for the evening, while lunch could consist of bread, cheese and fruit on the beach, or in a wayside field.

Sea food is the staple diet in Brittany and ranges from little shrimps, scallops and mussels, a variety of oysters from Concarneau, Cancale and the Morbihan, crabs, langoustine, and, of course, the lobster. That rich dish *hômard a l'Americaine* is a Breton dish, originally and still in Brittany correctly spelt *a l'Armorique.*

Brittany is also very much the country of the *crêpe,* or pancake. These have two varieties. The buckwheat *galette* is rolled around eggs, ham, cheese or any conceivable savoury filling. A *crêperie* in Vannes offers a choice of forty different fillings for your *galette.* The *crêpe,* on the other hand, made from plain wheat, is used as the base for a dessert dish, often with ice-cream. A swift, cheap, snack in a *crêperie* is the ideal lunch if you are visiting a town centre or want a quick meal when on the road.

Bretons are also very fond of pâtés and pies, which are both rich and inexpensive. *Andouillettes,* heavy thick sausages, are decidedly an acquired taste, but the *gigot pré-salé,* lamb reared on the salt marshes west of Mont-St-Michel, is really delicious. In St Malo,

the sea food platter, *assiette de fruit de mer,* is also delicious, but tends to be served in enormus portions. (I stayed late at one restaurant just to see if the gentleman at a neighbouring table could finish his dish, which consisted of lobster claws, a whole crab, twelve belon oysters, several langoustines and handfuls of assorted shell fish. When he had polished off the lot — washed down with a bottle of *Cidre bouché* — the pile of debris on his side-plate was nearly a foot high!)

Fish of all kinds is frequently featured either as a soup or a stew. The local version of *bouillabaisse* is called the *cotriade,* and the locals say this is best served at Larmour, a fishing village, below Lorient. Trout is good anywhere in the Argoat, while at Châteaulin the salmon is excellent, notably at the *Ducs de Lin,* on the road to Quimper. Breton vegetables are excellent. It has been truly said that one measure of a good cook is the way in which he handles vegetables, and by that standard, Breton cooking is excellent indeed.

When the time comes, you may be too full for pudding, but apart from the ritual chant 'glacé - fruit - flan - fromage - tarte-au-chocolate etc' the Bretons have their crêpe and such local dishes as *far,* a sort of sweet custard tart, excellent strawberries from the Plougastel peninsula, and the *quatre-quart* cake, with dried fruit and raisins, which goes very well with coffee.

As regards wine, there is Muscadet and very little else. Indeed wines from other regions seem distinctly expensive in Breton restaurants.

Muscadet comes from the pays Nantais, the region on the south bank of the Loire west of Nantes, and is a relatively recent wine, for no one drank Muscadet before World War I. It is the only wine which takes its name from the grape, rather than the region, like Beaujolais, Bordeaux or Burgundy. Muscadet is a dry, sharp, white wine and naturally complements the local fish and sea food and should be served very cold. Muscadet is best drunk young, and, if very young, within three months of the vintage, is called *Muscadet-sur-Lie.* In any event it should be drunk within two years, and if you take some bottles home, let it rest before you drink it. *Gros-plant* Muscadet, from the pays de Retz, again south of the Loire along the Sevre, can be bought by the case direct from the growers.

Wine apart, the Bretons drink vast quantities of cider. In the autumn the apple trees which dot the countryside are thick with the small scarlet cider apples, and the smell of apples from the piles in the farmyards is forever wafting in through the car window. Do not be diffident about ordering *cidre* with your meal, for you will quickly notice it on many tables and many Bretons actually prefer it to wine, even to their beloved Muscadet.

An hour out to sea off Lorient is the island of Groix. This is a steep-sided island with a considerable swell smashing against the cliffs even on the calmest day. There is only one port, Port Tudy, on the north shore, and from there it is a short walk across the island to see the great surfing waves foam in at Locmaria bay. The bird life is, as usual, very varied especially gannets which fold their wings high over the sea and plunge deeply into the waves. A visit to Groix takes only half-a-day and the island is most attractive and, out of season, quite deserted.

Back on the mainland and east of Port Louis lies the chapel of Merlévenez. This is one of the very few Romanesque churches in Brittany and even has those saw-toothed porches typical of the contemporary Norman architecture of England. Merlévenez will make you feel very much at home. Far stranger, however, is St Cado's chapel on an island over the estuary of the Etel, although this too is Romanesque, built by the Knights Templar in the very early years of the twelfth century.

St Cado was a Welsh saint, who came to Brittany in the sixth century. He eventually left his chapel here to become Bishop of Benevento, but not before he had persuaded the Devil (who must have been very gullible) to help him build the causeway which connects the chapel with the mainland. The deal called for the road to be built in one night and the price was to be the soul of the first living thing across. The Devil anticipated that St Cado himself would make the first trip, but the saint sent his cat across instead. The Devil then decided to breach the causeway, but St Cado kicked him into the sea, leaving his saintly footprint on the rocks in the process, where it can still be seen. There is a similar story told in Wales about the Devil's Bridge near Aberystwyth, where one Blodwin, sent her cow across to pay the Devil's price — and this is said to be the reason why cows have horns! The little island of St Cado is easily missed, but you will not regret going there.

Below St Cado, Etel is a port for tunny fishing, which is now a sport as well as an industry, while the estuary above Etel is a sheltered haven for many yachts.

The road south to Quiberon runs past the first of the Morbihan menhirs, near Kerzerho, and you can press on to stay in Plouharnel, and eat at the Kerank, or you can turn north to Auray and pass the night at the Hôtel des Voyageurs, before exploring the gulf of Morbihan, the mysteries of the menhirs of Carnac, and the varied islands of the inland sea.

6 Morbihan: Auray Quiberon & Vannes

Auray is one of the major towns around the Morbihan gulf and it comes as a considerable surprise to discover how small it is. The population barely exceeds eight thousand and it is, in reality, little more than a large village, famous today only for the pilgrim centre of Ste Anne d'Auray to the north and the beautiful *quartier* St Goustan, down by the river Loc.

The way down to the *quartier* is signposted in the town and you should make your first stop down there, on the *Quai* Franklin. Notice first the little Customs House on the bridge before you stroll down the *quai*. Here, on 4 December 1776, Benjamin Franklin came ashore, the first ambassador to France from the then rebel colonists of the United States. Franklin's ship had been prevented by foul winds from docking at Nantes and was diverted instead to the port of Auray. The choice of Franklin as ambassador was, in itself,

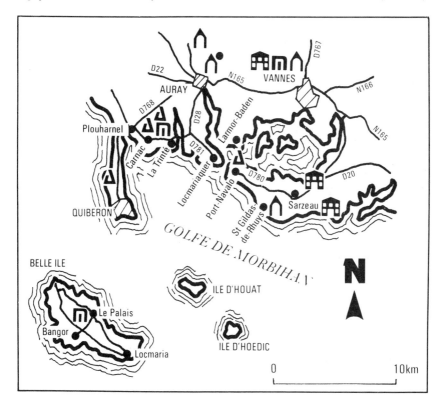

Franklin plaque, Auray

PLACES TO VISIT IN AND NEAR AURAY

The Chârtreuse d'Auray
Built on the battlefield of 1364, this Carthusian monastery is open daily.

St Goustan Quarter
Auray
An attractive part of the town, with many old houses, on the far side of the river.

Ste Anne d'Auray
A pilgrim centre, with regular 'pardons' throughout the year, and a large one on 26 July. See the Basilica, and the Treasury. Open: daily 10am-5pm.

extraordinary, for although he had signed the Declaration of Independence, he was best known in Europe as the inventor of the lightning conductor. This was hardly likely to impress the elegant court of Louis XVI, although Louis had watched with fascination when the first lightning conductor was installed at Marly in 1752 and during a storm 'drew sparks from the thunder'.

However, Franklin was popular at the French Court and was much admired for his simplicity and honest language, rare virtues there. He obtained subsidies and arms which enabled the thirteen colonies to survive until their victory over Burgoyne at Saratoga brought France openly on to their side.

Opposite the Quai Franklin is the start of the popular Auray promenade, which leads up the hill and gives excellent views over Auray and the Morbihan gulf. Notice, all along the river, the flat oyster platforms of the fishermen, for most of the oysters grown in Brittany are bred from 'spat' cultivated in the Morbihan. You can also take one of the Vedettes Verte boats out of Auray and tour the gulf itself.

The road north towards Ste Anne's crosses the marshy flood-plain where, on 29 September 1364, the two rival contenders for the dukedom, Charles of

Blois with Duguesclin, and Jean de Montfort with John Chandos, met in their last and decisive battle. Charles was defeated and killed on the field, and Duguesclin was captured. Jean was reportedly very upset at the death of his cousin and wept openly until John Chandos pointed out that many men had died to get him the dukedom and the death of his rival was not the greatest loss. Jean later built a chantry chapel and monastery on the battlefield, now the Chartreuse d'Auray, and a memorial to the Chouans.

Ste-Anne-d'Auray is not a medieval pilgrimage centre. It is still very much alive, and the procession there on 25 July is certainly the most popular pardon in Brittany. Ste Anne was the mother of Mary and she has always been a popular saint. The shrine at Auray was established in 1624 when a statue of Ste Anne was unearthed here, after a local man, Yves, had a vision and was then led to the site by a ghostly candle, held in an invisible hand. The cult continued to grow for the next two centuries and the

Stone alignments at Carnac

present basilica was erected in the 1870s. It is not particularly attractive, although designed to accommodate large numbers of pilgrims. Further chapels are spread over the surrounding park.

The roof of the nearby hospital still clearly bears a red cross, painted on it in the last war to warn off hostile aircraft, and a short distance away, is the interesting memorial on the Champs de Martyrs, to the Chouans shot after the abortive Quiberon battle of 1795.

The road to Carnac runs south-west like an arrow, from Auray to Plouharnel and quickly reaches the menhir *alignments,* focus of all attention in this part of the coast.

A menhir is a standing stone — the word derived from the Breton *maen* (stone) and *hir* (long). Although there

are menhirs all over France, and at many other places in Europe, they are most numerous at Carnac. Over 5,000 stones, of varying height, are arranged about the countryside there in long *alignements.*

There is nothing aimless about their distribution; they were erected with immense effort and for some definite purpose, but no one knows why or by whom. They certainly date from the Neolithic or New Stone Age, and perhaps the early Bronze Age, and so were there long before the Gauls arrived to found Armorica. Glyn Daniel, the noted British archaeologist, dates them at about 2,000BC, but they may be up to 1,000 years earlier.

As to their purpose, there is much speculation. It is generally conceded that their underlying purpose is religious rather than scientific, even though they may have been aligned in a manner which enabled primitive astrologers to fix the date of the summer solstice, or moon-phases, with a view to the correct commencement of religious rites. One recent theory, on the other hand, is that their purpose was entirely scientific, and that they were used for astronomy, though to what use a Neolithic man could put such knowledge, even if he had it, has yet to be explained. Whatever their purpose, the menhirs of Carnac are a unique spectacle and draw visitors from all over the world, amazed at their number and the precise way in which they flow away over the fields. Seen on a misty autumn morning, they appear like a frozen army, while by moonlight they are weird indeed.

In Carnac *ville,* just past the High St Michel tumulus, is the Prehistoric Museum, established in about 1880 by James Miln, a Scotsman from Forfar. Miln could have lived in an earlier age, when amateurism was no barrier to expertise. He began life in the Royal Navy, then became a trader in the East. He studied astronomy, photography and archaeology, and spent seven years at Carnac, when, following this last pursuit to its conclusion, he founded the museum. It contains some of the many finds he made during his excavations.

If the purpose of the *alignements* is still unexplained, knowledge of the people who erected them is also lacking. Their existence suggests a tightly-organized society of considerable size and wealth — but who they were and what became of them is still unknown, although there is no lack of speculation.

Of the three main *alignements* at Carnac, that at Menac is the biggest and longest, with 1,099 menhirs stretching for nearly three-quarters of a mile. The

---

PLACES TO VISIT AT CARNAC

Prehistory Museum
Close to the famous lines, a splendid museum, full of interesting artifacts.

Megalithic Lines
Europe's finest collection of standing stones, numbering several thousand. A complete tour will take a full day.

---

others, at Kermaria and Kerlescan, are smaller, but with higher stones, and with plenty of other stones scattered in the surrounding fields.

Before leaving Carnac, however, one should dine at least once at Chez Maryline on the main road, where the food and service are unforgettable, or, more expensively, at the classical Larn-Roz in the Avenue de la Poste, or, for a good basic meal, at La Bourriche near the beach.

You can spend a happy morning among the stone rows of Carnac, before departing south to the *presqu'ile* de Quiberon.

The name *presqu'ile* is exactly right, for an 'almost island' is what the Quiberon peninsula has now become. It was originally a true island, but the neck of land has slowly silted up and a causeway through Penthièvre now leads swiftly across to this most attractive (almost) island.

At Kerhostin, turn off right on minor roads for the Pointe du Percho, and so down the Côte-Sauvage. On this very rugged coastline the waves really beat in tall combers with spindrift smoking off the top as they thunder in to the beaches and rocks. Swimming is hazardous here, for the undertows are treacherous. Even fishing can be dangerous, for a sudden extra-large wave has snatched many fishermen away from a seemingly secure

La Trinite-sur-Mer, Morbihan

place on the rocks.

This road leads down to the lovely little towns of Port Maria and Quiberon *ville.* You would do well to stay in the Hôtel de La Mer by the port. In the centre of Quiberon is a statue to General Hoche, who defeated a 'Chouan' force here in June 1795.

There was, at the time, a civil war in this part of France, between the Catholic pro-Royalist 'Chouans' and the Republican forces under Hoche. A British squadron landed an *emigré* force from England on Carnac beach, where they were quickly joined by more rebels from the interior. General Hoche, the Military Governor of Vannes, quickly defeated them, however. Those who fled and were not speedily evacuated by the British Fleet, were rounded up and shot at Chartreuse, north of Auray. This English defeat served as some small compensation for the defeat of the French Fleet in Quiberon Bay by Hawke and the capture of Belle-Ile by the Royal Marines in 1761, a triumph the Royal Corps still hold as a battle honour. It was to celebrate these successes that David Garrick wrote the 'Hearts of Oak' march for the Royal Navy.

From Port Maria a ferry goes over to that most famous island, an hour's journey offshore. Belle-Isle was only briefly in British hands, for it was exchanged for Nova Scotia in 1763. It had once been owned by Nicolas Fouquet, Chief Minister to the young Louis XIV. Fouquet had fortified the island in case the king learnt of his speculations. He intended to flee there and wait out the storm, but his arrest was too sudden and he lived out his days in the dungeons of Vincennes. His family retained the island until the British arrived, and in the eighteenth century it became quite fashionable.

Sarah Bernhardt had a summer home there on the Pointe des Poulains, and the island is still popular with the famous. It is not too large, about thirty square miles, and the 'capital', Le Palais, is quite charming. The smaller islands to the east, Houat and Hoedic, can also be visited.

The Quiberon peninsula shelters the bay from the westerly gales and provides a very large and sheltered anchorage, very popular with yachts. There are also some excellent long sandy beaches popular for 'sand' yachting, notably by Port Haliguen, and there are more menhirs near St Pierre.

Before returning through Auray, go west again across the Crac'h estuary and down to Locmariaquer to see the 'Great Menhir' and the 'Table des Marchands'. The Great Menhir was struck by lightning and now lies on the ground, broken into four huge parts. It was once called the *Men-er-Roec'h,* the Fairy Wand. The dolmen of the 'Table des Marchands' is a little to the rear and covers a grave. Notice the carvings on one of the upright stones just inside the entrance.

Locmariaquer is the nearest place to the western shore of the gap through which the sea surges into the Gulf de Morbihan, and you can take a boat from here to tour the Gulf — but be sure it returns here. If it lands on the far shore, it is a long walk back.

The advice on keeping to minor roads has advantages, for, if you take the little road south from Auray towards Larmor-Baden to tour around the Gulf, you will come out up on the hill and can look down from there on the little port at Bono, a veritable gem.

From the road bridge above the town you look directly down on the town, with the viaduct, spanning the river, picked out against the hundreds of whitewashed tiles stacked along the quay. These are used to gather the oyster 'spat', and it is a good point at which to reflect on the curious sex life of the oyster. Once upon a time oysters bred all round the Breton coast, but ever-increasing pollution and a serious disease has restricted the main breeding ground to the Gulf of Morbihan, from which most oyster embryos come. Brittany has three types of oysters. There is firstly, the huge Cancale, from the north coast, about the size of a saucer. Next is the *belons,* from Finistère, and lastly the *portugaises,* though they do not come from Portugal. None of them contains pearls. The oyster is bi-sexual and self-fertilising, changing sex from male to female as necessary. Basically, the oyster larvae or 'spat' are first grown on hollow, curved

tiles, like those to be seen at Bono. They develop for about six months in shallow water until they are ready to be bedded out in the deeper, but richer waters, exposed to the open sea. As they stay there for about three years before being cropped, the oysters are about three-and-a-half, to four years old when eaten.

If, nevertheless, you still cherish an appetite for them, hurry on to the Hôtel Parc-Fétan, a Logis de France hotel at Larmor-Baden, with fine views over the Morbihan and out towards the largest of the many islands in the gulf, the Isle-aux-Moines, 'Monks Island'.

The Isle-aux-Moines can be reached from the little port of Port Blanc, north of Larmor-Baden, two hundred metres across the glittering waters. One can cruise all over the gulf in the ferry-boats of the Vedettes-Vertes line, and no visit

Dolmen de l'Ile aux Moines

to the Morbihan is complete without a trip on one of their vessels, which can be joined at a score of landing stages.

The Gulf of Morbihan covers an area of over 1,000 square miles, and the sea floods into it between Port Navolo and Kerpenhir, through a gap only 600m wide. The tides and current are, therefore, high and fast-flowing, the tidal height being about sixteen feet. There are scores of islands within the Gulf; allegedly one for every day of the year. Forty of them are inhabited, of which the largest is the Isle-aux-Moines.

the Hôtel le Roof, on the little island of Conleau, south of the city, and the embarkation point for another major Morbihan island, the Isle d'Arz, before continuing a tour of the Gulf.

Vannes is another place that *must* be visited. The old town is a walled city and the walls are ideal, turreted, with machicolations, a real taste of the knightly age. It is best to drive directly down to the harbour and park there, walking up towards the town and the Porte St Vincent, which is dominated by the statue of the Spanish saint, St Vincent-Ferrier, who died in the town in 1419. Before entering his gate, however, bear right, following the walls, for a first spectacular view of the ramparts, seen across the formal gardens and the Rohan river which serves the town as a moat.

Walk up towards the Porte Poterne and enter the town there, looking down to the old houses and *lavoir,* the washing places beneath the gateway, before entering the cobbled streets of this, the ancient capital of the Breton Kingdom.

This was the home of the Veneti, who were defeated by Decimus Brutus and then enslaved by Caesar — their tribal name alone remains and is commemorated at Vannes. In 826 the war-chief Nominöe, became Duke of Brittany, although he was, in all but name, an undisputed sovereign. He gave Brittany the frontiers which it kept until the Revolution of 1789 and chose Vannes as his capital. The city, which gained its cathedral in the 1200s, continued to be the centre for Breton affairs until 1532 when the Estates of Brittany accepted the marriage of Claude of Brittany and François of Angoulême as marking the permanent union of Brittany with the realm of France, so ending the Duchy's

The women of this island are reputed to be remarkably beautiful. It once belonged to a religious order, and as it covers an area of 25 square miles it was a considerable fief.

Returning to the mainland head north for Vannes, but stay at another Logis, existence as a separate power.

Vannes is full of attractions. The cathedral of St Pierre stands amid a network of old streets, now free of cars and still lined with leaning, crooked medieval houses, notably in the Rue de la Monnaie. On one, are the plump, grinning gargoyles, known as 'Vannes-and-his-Wife' and, outside the town-hall a fine armoured statue of the Constable de Richemont, brother of Duke John V, and uncle to that unhappy prince, Gilles de Bretagne, whom he tried to protect from his own folly and his brother's wrath. Richemont led the French Army which defeated the English under Talbot at Châtillon on the Dordogne, in 1453.

St Pierre, presently in the throes of cleaning and restoration, is a vast, echoing, gloomy place built as usual in the Flamboyant late-Gothic style. It contains the tomb of St Vincent, and there is an interesting treasury in the chapter house.

You can eat very well in Vannes at La Marée-Bleue, and stay, if not at Conleau, at the comfortable Marechaudière, but wherever you stay, Vannes, is a fine city.

Vannes lies at the head of the Morbihan gulf, and part of the southern arm of the gulf can be reached through Séné, although this road ends at the eastern arm of the gulf. By heading out on the Roche Bernard road and turning off left for Sarzeau, on the Rhuys peninsula, another name with a decidedly Welsh flavour, you will skirt this difficulty and still see the Gulf clearly, on your right.

This region, once forested, but now very bare, has several interesting sights and the first stop should be at the wonderful moated castle at Suscinio. This thirteenth-century castle was built as a summer residence for the Dukes of Brittany. Constable Richemont was born there and Bertrand Duguesclin laid siege to it in 1373, breaching the main curtain wall. The breach can still be identified by the paler stones used to fill it in after the castle was taken, and the English garrison put to the sword. The castle was besieged again during the Wars of Religion and then suffered the usual fate of medieval castles once their day was done, being gradually dismantled for its supply of dressed stone. Fortunately, this process was halted before it went too far and Suscinio — the Sans-Souci castle — is now being restored. A walk round the ramparts should only be attempted by those with a head for heights, since there is a giddy void on either side; a picnic lunch can be taken on the banks of the moat, or one can cross the main road to Sarzeau itself and dine at the Hôtel le Sage.

This is named from the town's most famous son, Alain-René le Sage, famous as the author of *Gil Blas*. Le Sage was born in 1688 and *Gil Blas,* a comedy of manners set in Spain and rather heavy going, is sometimes hailed as the first ever 'modern' French novel. Le Sage was the son of a lawyer and earned his first money as a translator of Spanish books, gaining thereby the background he needed for *Gil Blas,* before he left for Paris and a life of minor fame.

A more enduring name is recalled down the little road to the monastery of St Gildas du Rhuys, where, in about 1136, Abélard, the lover of Héloise, was appointed abbot. In his time, Abélard enjoyed — and clearly relished — considerable fame as a teacher and a conversationalist. A Breton, born at La Palet, near Nantes, in 1079 he went to Paris to study at the Schools, and quickly came to the attention of his teachers and fellow students, mainly because of his incisive intellect and

Moated castle at Suscinio

considerable charm. Abélard questioned, at first gently, and then directly, the established doctrines of the Church, and since radicals are always popular, at least with the young, he soon attracted a considerable following. He also attracted the attention of Canon Fulbert, of Notre-Dame, who had a daugher, Héloise. Héloise was not only beautiful but also extremely intelligent. Fulbert is a much-maligned man, but he cannot have been an unthinking brute, for, in an age when women were merely chattels, he had educated Héloise carefully, and he wanted Abélard, the star of Paris, to become her tutor. Abélard moved into the canon's house and the couple quickly became lovers, but when Héloise became pregnant, she refused to marry him, leaving him to live with his mother in Brittany and bear a son who was given the unusual name of

Astrolaube. Meanwhile, Canon Fulbert was, not without reason, highly incensed. He had invited Paris's leading intellectual into his home, where he had promptly debauched his daughter, then failed to marry her, and was now seemingly unrepentant. In the face of his mounting rage, the couple decided to marry, but in secret, which failed to satisfy Canon Fulbert, who wanted his daughter's belated respectability to become widely known, and, finally goaded beyond endurance, he hired some bully-boys to break into Abélard's lodgings and castrate him!

French farce had turned into tragedy and it is on their subsequent sad lives that the love story of Abélard and Héloise has been based. The couple parted, Abélard to the Abbey at St Denis and Héloise into various convents, but they corresponded regularly and their love letters have since become classics. To fill his time and quieten his mind, Abélard then delved even deeper and with increasing dissatisfaction into the doctrines of the Church, and in so doing met with increasing opposition. To lie low for a while, he accepted the position of abbot at the remote monastery of St Gildas, but his choice of refuge proved far from happy. The monks were rebellious and far from impressed with his intellect, while the country people were savage and hostile.

'I find myself,' he wrote to Héloise, 'still in danger, a sword forever over my head. I live in a wild country where every day brings new perils.' The monks tried several times to poison him, and he finally fled from the abbey by night and made his way to shelter at Cluny. His time at St Gildas had not been completely wasted. He established a nunnery at the Paraclete, and installed Héloise there as abbess, and finally

---

PLACES TO VISIT IN VANNES

Prehistoric Museum
Château-Gailliard, Vannes,
A fine collection of prehistoric,
Gallo-Roman and medieval exhibits,
from local excavations.

St Peter's Cathedral
A very fine Gothic cathedral, with an interesting treasury, open mid-July - mid-September. The cathedral has the tomb of St Vincent Ferrier.

Boat trips in the Morbihan
Around the Morbihan on the boats of the Vedettes-Verte to the Ile-aux-Moines.

To Belle-Isle from Quiberon.

---

composed his concerns about the Church into a tract, *Sic-en-Non* which was published in 1139. The root of Abélard's doubts lay in his opposition to the doctrine of St Anselm 'Through faith shall ye come to understanding.' Abélard, an intelligent man, could not accept this, and made a counter-propostion, 'I must understand in order that I may believe' and ran headlong against the disciplines of the Church.

St Bernard of Clairvaux attacked Abélard fiercely and in 1140 brought him before a Council of the Church at Sens, where he was roundly condemned. His writings were seized and burned as works tainted with heresy, and only the protection of Peter the Venerable, Abbot of Cluny, saved him from ending his days in a church prison, 'eating the bread of repentance, and drinking the waters of affliction', or even at the stake.

Worn out with his life, which had begun so splendidly and was spent in conflict, he returned to Cluny where he died in 1142. Héloise lived on until 1163 and died at the Paracléte, after which their bodies were brought together at the Père-Lachaise cemetery in Paris, 'where, beyond these voices, there is peace.'

St Gildas is a small town, dominated by the church and cloisters of the old abbey. It was largely rebuilt in the seventeenth century, but much of the Romanesque features of Abélard's day still survive, notably in the chancel, and it still holds some interesting objects.

The presbytery contains various relics including the limbs of St Gildas, a Welsh saint who sailed across to Rhuys in the seventh century. His abbey was burned by the Northmen and re-established by St Felix, who built the abbey which Abélard knew. The abbey was the burial place for the ducal family of Brittany, should any of them die at Suscinio, and several members of the family, notably children, are buried there.

In the summer sun it is hard to find in St Gildas the gloomy spiteful monastery of Abélard's writings, but it can be a bleak spot in winter, when the gales blow in past Belle-Ile and sweep the grey town with salty rain.

Further on, towards the tip of the peninsula, near Port-Navalo, on the right is a tall barrow, the 'Tumulus of Thumiac' from which Caesar is said to have watched Brutus defeat the Veneti. They were sea-faring folk, with strong, sturdy sailing ships, and Brutus sailed against them in light, oared galleys, taking advantage of a windless day and hurling sickles into their rigging to bring down their masts. Once the Roman soldiers could board the Veneti ships and fight hand-to-hand, victory was certain. After the battle, all the Veneti warriors were slaughtered, and their

GOOD BEACHES IN MORBIHAN

Quiberon peninsular
Carnac
Bénodet
Etel, west of Auray
Locmariaquer

women and children sold into slavery. From this mound Caesar could see all this, and if you climb up on top today, there is the sea-coast to the south, and to the right, the Gulf of Morbihan, laid out before you. Go there at evening and sit on top to watch the sun go down. It sinks slowly and then seems to plunge into the western sky, filling the bay with deep purple shadows, while vast flocks of pink-tipped gulls rise from the flooding sand-banks and wheel away to the north.

St Gildas

7 The Eastern Morbihan: Josselin to La Rochebernard___

North of Vannes lies rolling country, straddled east and west by the escarpment of the Landes de Lanvaux, which begin near Baud in the west and peter out near Rochefort-en-Terre. This area is frequently described in guidebooks as a moorland, but it is now intensively cultivated and consists mainly of rich farmland, although the odd patch of ferny heath and rocky outcrop can still be found.

A little above Vannes, in a wooded dale, you will come to the towers of Elven. These are the remains of a château-fort built in the thirteenth century and later owned by the Lord of Rieux, who was tutor to the Duchesse Anne. The castle was destroyed in 1488 by the troops of Charles VIII, but there are still considerable remains, including the central keep and two gateways. For two years, between 1474 and 1476, it was the prison of Henry Tudor, Duke of Richmond, who later overthrew Richard III on Bosworth Field and became Henry VII of England.

Bear off northwards here, on minor roads, and head towards Trédion, on the

Towers of Elven

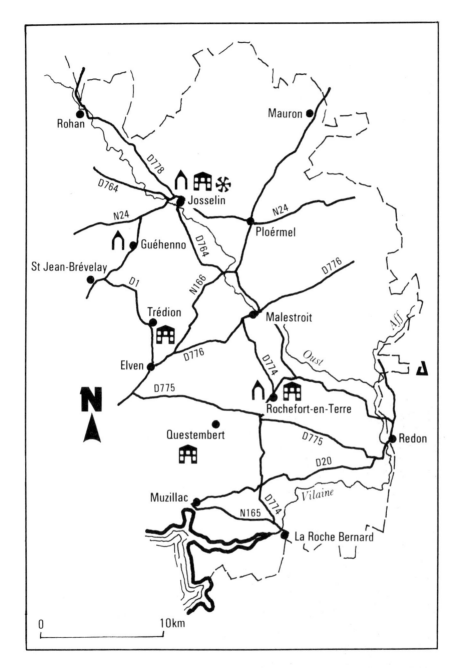

Lanvaux moors. This countryside is
dotted with menhirs and megalithic
remains while at Trédion, an attractive

little place, there is a wide lake fronting a
thick-walled medieval manor house.
This is virtually on the crest of the

Calvary at Guehénno

Lanvaux, with good views to the north, and the road dips down to the valley of the Claie, and leads north to Guehénno.

Guehénno has a calvary, one of the few to be found in the Morbihan. It dates from the mid-sixteenth century, but has been restored in the last hundred years. The central cross has two cross-members, and the lower half of the monument carries statues of four apostles. The column in the foreground, bears a carving of the cock which witnessed the denials of Peter.

To the north again, Josselin is one of the most famous towns of Brittany and seat of the Rohan family.

> *Roi ne puis,*
> *Prince ne daigne,*
> *Rohan suis.*

Or, in English:

> *King I am not,*
> *Prince I wouldn't deign to be,*
> *I am the Lord de Rohan.*

St Nazaire U-boat pen entrance

Vitré Castle

Chateau de la Bretesche

There is so much to see in Josselin that it is hard to know where to start, but since the castle dominates the town, drive down to the river Oust, now a canal and start from there, where the great castle walls, built on solid rock, rear up high overhead. The river once ran hard against the walls, making Josselin theoretically impregnable, but a road runs there now and from the towpath there are fine views of the castle.

The castle consists of a curtain wall on the river side, dropping downhill at the rear, towards the village centre. The castle is still inhabited and remains in the possession of the Rohan family, who have owned it since the Middle Ages.

The original castle was built about 1,000 AD by Guéthenoc, Count of Porhoët, and was named after his second son, Josselin. Continually modified for the next four hundred years, in 1168 it withstood a siege by Henry II of England, who was ravaging the lands of those Bretons still resisting the lordship of his son Geoffrey. Henry eventually took the place and destroyed both castle and township. It was rebuilt about 1175 and survived the Hundred Years' War, when from 1370 it was held by Oliver de Clisson. His daughter married into the Rohan family and took the castle as her dowry. A dowry was usually a house or land, provided by the bride's family to support their daughter in her old age, when her husband had died and she became a 'dowager'.

The castle was 'slighted', that is, the fortifications were overthrown, in the sixteenth century, on the orders of Richelieu, and during the Revolution the family fled abroad and did not return until 1860. Since then, much time and money has been spent restoring the castle, and filling it with antiques and art treasures. It can be visited, and one exhibit of particular interest is the table on which Henry IV signed the Edict of Nantes, on 13 August 1598.

The Rohans, certainly in pre-Revolutionary days, were a very wealthy family with vast estates in France, notably in Anjou, and abroad. Like all old families they have had their share of statesmen and rogues and one son, of a minor branch of the house, in the eighteenth century, was the Prince de Rohan, a very worldly cleric and cardinal of Strasbourg. De Rohan met Marie-Antoinette and her formidable mother, Maria-Theresa, when he was appointed ambassador to the Hapsburg Court at Vienna. His ostentatious dress, gambling and general wildness made a most regrettable impression on the Hapsburg Court and, when Marie-Antoinette became Queen of France, the cardinal's future looked bleak indeed.

De Rohan had a capacity for making unfortunate friends and he had in his train none other than the necromancer and confidence trickster, Cagliostro. No more discreet, the queen numbered among her ladies, Jeanne de la Motte, a descendant of the Valois kings. It so happened that a Paris jeweller had for sale a necklace valued at the huge sum of a thousand livres and, although the queen refused to let the king buy it for her, saying that for that money they could build a battleship, Cagliostro and Jeanne conspired together to convince the cardinal that she was really desperate to have it and that if he bought the necklace and presented it to the queen, his future would at once become bright with promise.

The cardinal purchased the necklace and gave it to Jeanne, who, instead of passing it on to the queen, made off with it. Jeanne broke the necklace up and sold the jewels to shops all over Paris. Some of the diamonds may still be found

Château de Josselin

on the ears and necks of French nobility. The cardinal, meanwhile, was waiting anxiously for a delighted letter from the queen and eventually, when it failed to arrive, the whole story came out. The queen was less than pleased to find her name involved in a confidence trick. The conspirators were caught and, together with the cardinal, flung into the Bastille. After a very brief trial Jeanne was branded and imprisoned. Cagliostro — who had played a very minor role, was censured and deported, and the cardinal was banished to the remote and chilling monastery of La Chaise-Dieu in the Auvergne, a long way from the glittering, if doomed, court of the later Bourbons.

The township of Josselin is small, with little more than two thousand people, but it is a medieval gem, full of leaning timbered houses. You can walk down the hill of the Rue du Trente, on the way to the little chapel of Notre Dame du Roncier, 'Our Lady of the Brambles', and see the houses as you pass.

Our Lady of the Brambles has a pardon on the second Sunday in September — she is the patroness of epileptics. The shrine dates to the fifteenth century when a peasant, cutting back the brambles in his fields, found a statue of the Virgin. He carried it home but that night it disappeared from his fireside and was found next day once again back among the thorns. This happened several times, until a sanctuary was built on the saint's chosen piece of ground. The original statue, which must have been quite large, was burned by the mob in 1793, but the charred fragment which remains, and a new statue, are still the centre for the annual pilgrimage. The shrine is below ground level and, as is quite usual with Breton shrines, is on the site of a spring.

Back in the town stands the enormous church of Notre-Dame-du-Roncier, founded in about 1100 and crowned with a great bell-tower. On a Sunday the bells above go full-blast, the air near the church is almost visibly full of their thunderous clamour. Inside the church is the tomb of Oliver de Clisson, who died at Josselin in 1407, and his wife Marguerite de Rohan, the first châtelain of the castle.

During one period of the Hundred Years' War and during the time of the more local War of the Breton Succession, the seneschal of the castle was a Breton, Jean de Beaumanoir, who held the castle for the Countess of Penthièvre of the Blois faction, and warred with the rival English garrison at nearby Plöermel, holding their castle for the de Montforts. In March 1351, close to Easter and time for the Peace of God,

PLACES TO VISIT IN THE EASTERN MORBIHAN

Josselin Castle
Josselin
Home of the Rohans, and a magnificent castle.

Chapel, Our Lady of the Rosebush
(Notre-Dame-de-Roncier), Josselin
Site of a great annual pardon on 2 September.

Site of the Battle of the Thirty
Midway between Josselin and Plöermel. Scene of the tournament of 1351.

Old Houses
La Roche-Bernard
The attractive sixteenth- and seventeenth-century houses in the Ruicard quarter are worth seeing.

a truce was declared among the rival parties, which did not please Jean de Beaumanoir at all.

On the evening of 26 March, he arrived before the walls of Plöermel with a herald and, on being admitted, made a startling proposal to the English knights of the garrison and their leader, Richard Bambro.

He challenged them to meet with the thirty knights of Josselin on the following day, at a point mid-way between the two castles, and fight to the death with sharpened weapons. His challenge was accepted and the English knights, reinforced by some German men-at-arms to make up the numbers,

---

CASTLES IN THE MORBIHAN

Lovers of medieval fortifications will enjoy the following castles:

Josselin
Vannes
Kerlevenan
Suscinio
Berric
Rochefort-en-Terre

---

rode off to the Mi-Voie oak on the following day and met the knights of Josselin. The fight made a great stir in Western Europe and was recounted in Froissart's Chronicles. As the combatants were all mercenary captains, professional soldiers, and not romantically-inclined knight-errants, both the offer and acceptance were surprising, particularly when the Plöermel faction included some simple men-at-arms in their ranks, a breach in the knightly code.

This combat, the *Combat-de-Trente,* or Battle of the Thirty, was illegal under the terms of the truce, as it took place

during one of those periodic pauses in strife often imposed at the time of religious festivals such as Christmas and Easter. Presented as a tournament, it was, however, widely regarded as an extremely chivalrous encounter, and those participants who survived escaped excommunication and gained much glory, although the death toll was high and the purpose of the fight was slaughter.

The knights fought on foot, with sword, axe, mace and spear. The fighting went on all day, with pauses for refreshment, until the knights were completely exhausted. The combat finished when a Breton knight mounted and rode his charger through the remaining English knights, knocking them to the ground. The outcome was total victory for the Bretons of Blois, eight Englishmen (including Bambro) being killed, and the rest made prisoner. There is a vivid account of this fight in Arthur Conan Doyle's historical romance *Sir Nigel.*

To see the Battlefield of the Thirty you must go out towards Plöermel, past the site and then turn back in the direction of Josselin, for the road is a dual-carriageway, and the site cannot be reached from the west-to-east lane. The field is a wide glade surrounded by tall trees, and a high obelisk, erected by Louis XVIII dominates the centre of the square. Behind the obelisk is a much smaller and much older cross, where some almost indecipherable carving records the name of Beaumanoir.

The plaque on the main obelisk is a little ironic. It records the names of the Breton Knights, but concludes *'Vive le Roi longtemps, les Bourbons toujours!'* A family, of which it was well said, that they learned nothing and forgot nothing, are now themselves almost forgotten.

The town of Plöermel, about eight

Site of the Battle of the Thirty

---

miles from Josselin, is a little larger. It was once the seat of the Dukes of Brittany, but their castle, the one from which Bambro marched his men to the combat, has long since disappeared. There are still traces of the old town walls and in several places they have been converted into the outer wall of houses, high on the ramparts, the gaps in the machicolations, between the merlons, serving as windows.

In the Rue Beaumanoir is the Maison des Marmousets, carved with caryatides, and the town has several fine old buildings. The church of St Armel is interesting for the carvings on the doorways, and inside are the tombs of two Dukes, Jean II and Jean III. A little way east of Plöermel lies the moated manor of Trécesson, on the edge of Paimpont and the Val-Sans-Retour, but for the moment let us stay in the Morbihan.

You can stay very comfortably near Plöermel in the Relais du Val d'Aoust, at La Chapelle, or back in Josselin at the Hôtel du Château, on the banks of the Oust, and turn your thoughts away from the wars and once again towards food.

While always good, and frequently excellent, Breton food is sometimes a little predictable. It is firmly based on the produce of the sea and if you spend a long time there, you can feel in need of a change. Throughout France, as nowhere else in Europe, the variety of the cuisine is remarkable, and it has acquired a new dimension within the last thirty years with the arrival of the Vietnamese from the former French colony of Indo-China.

Vietnamese restaurants are found all over France, and their cooking should not be confused with that of the Chinese.

Many find Vietnamese food delicious, more delicate and *raffinée* than Chinese, and served in more sensible portions, although there are some superficial simularities. All Vietnamese dishes are served in small portions or slices, and you eat with chopsticks; even as the French eat everything with bread, and the Belgians eat everything with chips, all Vietnamese main dishes are served with rice.

A typical Vietnamese meal begins with soup, or crab-meat, shrimps, beef, pork or duck, all sliced and mixed with rice or two kinds of noodle, the clear noodle from the soya bean, or rice noodles. As an alternative to a soup, try a salad with mixed vegetables, mixed again with shrimps, chicken or crab.

Then, a real Vietnamese speciality, try the *Nems,* small crisp spring-rolls, stuffed with pork or crab. These little thumb-size rolls are now very popular in France and quite delicious. Main dishes include *Shop-Soy,* sliced meat or shrimps with vegetables; *Mi-xao,* meat with fried noodles; *Canard-Laque,* crisp fried duck; or *Riz-Cantonais,* a mixture of rice, ham, shrimps and egg. These dishes are accompanied by three kinds of sauce, the usual soya bean sauce, a fish sauce, and a very hot pepper-sauce. The dessert is lycheés or fruit, and the usual drink is jasmine tea.

Turning away south, towards the coast, you cross the Lanvaux 'moor', through Malestroit, down to the town of Rochefort-en-Terre, a little town full of curious treasures and in many ways quite extraordinary.

It stands on the bluff, overlooking a rocky part of the Lanvaux, and contains the restored thirteenth-century castle of Rochefort, destroyed by the Catholic League in 1594, again by the Chouans in 1793 and finally rebuilt in the present century. This castle is a private home and can rarely be visited, but one can go down and look at the carvings on the postern gate. This is divided into twelve panels showing knights, saints and apostles, and is really quite a work of art, a memorable little treasure.

The main street, or Grande Rue, which leads back from the castle, is full of fine houses, all painted white, and raised up a little above the street level. Notice the hanging signs outside the shops and the carvings on the door panels of the inns and restaurants, a feature of Rochefort-en-Terre.

A little downhill, in a square, lies the church of Notre-Dame-de-la-Tronchaye, squat, grey building, with tombs outside the south door, and its nave of the church below ground level; on entering the church, you go down a flight of six steps.

The statue of Our Lady seems to be very old, a Black Virgin, said to date from before the time of the Northmen. Discovered in a hollow tree (or *tronchaye*) in the twelfth century, it has a pardon on the third Sunday in August. This ornate church is full of late medieval curiosities and well worth a visit. You can eat well in Rochefort at the Café Breton and stay at the Hostellérie du Lion d'Or in the Grande Rue. If you feel like a stop in really luxurious surroundings, you can travel a little way south to the three-star Hôtel de Bretagne at Questembert.

From Rochefort go east, to Redon, not for the town itself, but because it stands on the Vilaine and you can visit the rather fine collections of dolmens, menhirs and megaliths at St-Just, a little way to the north. This lies, however, outside the Morbihan, in Ille-et-Vilaine, so let us turn south and follow the river, the boundary of the *département* of Morbihan, south towards the sea.

At La Roche-Bernard they used to

build ships in the seventeenth century, it has now become little more than a tourist resort and a yachting centre. The town is overlooked by the new high suspension bridge which carries the main Vannes to Nantes road and gives, fine, if giddy, views up the river valley and to the south-east. a first glimpse of the marshland of Brière, the next stop.

Here, on the Vilaine, we have to leave the Morbihan, with considerable regret. The Morbihan contains all that is best and most interesting in Brittany, a district full of history and colour, with fine food and good weather besides. Still, do not be despondent, the future is still promising and, after all, we can always come back.

8 Loire-Atlantique: The Briere, Nantes, Châteaubriant

The Vilaine divides the Morbihan from the eastern *département* of Loire-Atlantique and officialdom has widened the breach by detaching this *département* from Brittany and including it in the newly created region of 'Pays de la Loire'. We are therefore stretching the boundary, but only a trifle, when we include this area in a book on modern Brittany.

By decree, therefore, Brittany shrinks, but in reality nothing has changed and, in any case, all this has happened before, and with very little effect. Some say that Brittany once extended south across the Loire into the Pays de Retz, which most people would include in the Vendée. Loire-Atlantique began as Loire-Inferieure, before the Bretons decided that such a title did little for their *amour-propre*, and had it changed.

The weird flatlands of the Brière are different, the Camargue of Northern France, a waste of marshes and canals, tall grass and reed-beds, lonely, haunting, and strange. Do not miss them.

The Brière lies south, beyond the road between la Roche-Bernard and Nantes, and to reach the heart of the area turn off at the Château de la Bretesche at Missillac, which is quite beautiful, and head across country on minor roads to la Chapelle-des-Marais and St Joachim.

The word *marais*, or marsh, betrays the origins of this country. It was formerly a great bog, a region of sandbanks and salt marsh, now drained by canals, but some of the marsh still remains in the very south of the area, around Guérande.

The centre of the Brière is the island of Fédrun and from there, in the village, you can take one of the black flat-bottomed punts called *chalands* or *blains,* and pole away along the canals. But there is not much to see as the grass towers high overhead and the wildlife seems sparse. The scattered houses are mud-walled, whitewashed and heavily thatched, not unlike the cottages one finds in the remote parts of Ireland or the Scottish Highlands. Many are now in ruins, for the native population is withering away and the canals are slowly silting up for lack of use.

For over three hundred years, this was the home of a dour and secretive people, who made a bare living by herding sheep, wildfowling, and cutting and selling the peat. The Brière belongs to the residents of the surrounding communes who alone have the right to cut peat there, and even they only for a frantic nine days in August. The people and the region have been immortalised in a book by Alphonse de Châteaubriand.

Today, many local people work in the dockyards at St Nazaire and in 1970 the region was declared a regional park. Since that time it has enjoyed a mild revival, and as the increasing income — one can hardly say wealth — of the local people has led to a decline in indiscriminate shooting, the population of marsh birds, for which this is a superb habitat, is now on the increase. At

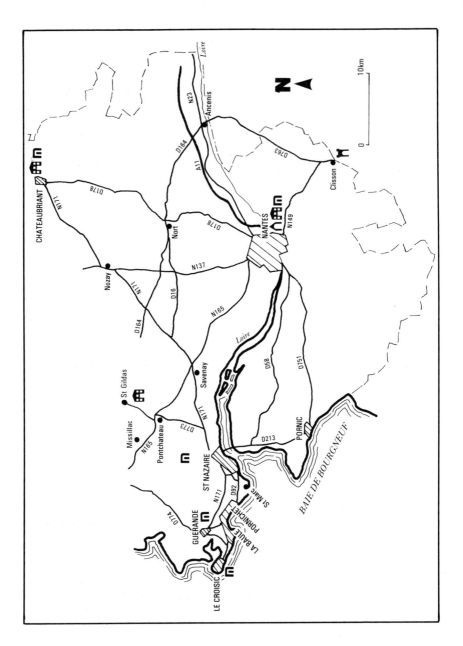

Fédrun there is a Park Museum, and an excellent restaurant, the Auberge du Parc, where the food tries hard to justify the price and almost succeeds.

The park covers most of a vast

headland between the Vilaine and the Loire and you can go south still further through the Porte St Michel and into Guérande. Guérande is a disappoint-ment. It has been described as the

'Carcassone of the North', a fairly serious exaggeration. It is a small walled city, over-looking the grasslands to the north, and the marshlands to the south. There is a good view of the country from the top of the main gateway, the Porte St Michel, which contains another excellent folklore museum. Here, in 1365, was signed the Treaty of Guérande, which healed the breach between the rival claimants to the Duchy and enabled the Dukes to free themselves from the embrace of the English, and reaffirm their loyalty to France.

The Guérande peninsula is composed of the two arms of Croisic bay, which is slowly silting up and being drained as sheep pasture. Before long, it may be possible to drive right round the shore from the point at Piriac-sur-Mer to the Pointe du Croisic. At present, however, one must cross the causeway at Saille and go through Batz, along the coast, past the ruins of many windmills and so into Croisic.

Croisic is a fascinating place, where one can wander round the harbour, eat in the many excellent restaurants, notably Chez Nous on the *quai* Lenigo, or watch the tide flood in through the narrow gap between the port and Penbron opposite. The town has many fine buildings, dating from the sixteenth and seventeenth centuries when the town was an important port. The harbour, divided into three sections, with large colourful trawlers drawn up on the slips, is a great centre for the sardine industry.

The town hall is a maritime museum, as is only proper, for this was the home of Hervé Riel, the pilot who led the French fleet to safety after their defeat in a battle off La Hogue, Riel was a pressed man, and in gratitude for his help and skill, the French admiral, D'Amfreville, offered him any reward he wanted. Riel asked simply for a short spell of leave to

PLACES TO VISIT IN LOIRE ATLANTIQUE

Brière Marshland
Tours into the Brière Park, by boat, from Fédrun. Enquire at Maison du Parc, Fédrun.

Château de la Bretesche
Splendid moated castle, close to St Guildas.

Le Croisic
The fishing port of Le Croisic is a splendid place, well worth a visit.

Guérande
A walled town close to Le Croisic. See the museum in St Michel's Gate.

see his wife, Aurore, an event celebrated by Robert Browning in a rather uneven poem:

Names and deed alike are lost,
Note a pillar nor a post,
In his Croisic keeps alive the feat as it
    befell;
Not a head in white or black,
On a single fishing smack,
In memory of the man but for whom all
    had gone to wrack .... ·

Well, not in Browning's day perhaps, but there is a memorial now on the Grande Côte and an excessive number of Breton yachts, fishing boats and small crafts seem to be called *La Belle Aurore.*

Along the coast, east of Le Croisic, lies the large and popular resort of La Baule, like Dinard, its rival on the North Coast, a fashionable spot for the wealthy folk of France and the jaded appetites of *Tout-Paris.*

The beach at La Baule runs for three miles, a multi-coloured parade of red tents and bathers in summer, while yachts and windsurfers cavort in the blue seas beyond. It seems a million miles away from the desolate Brière or the work-a-day folk of Le Croisic.

La Baule is full of fine restaurants and although some may prefer the more simple *ambiance* of Le Croisic, you will eat excellently at l'Espadon in the Avenue Plage, or less expensively at the Châlet-Suisse. Pornichet was once separate from La Baule, but has now been completely absorbed by the larger resort, although it still retains its country market on Wednesdays and Sundays.

If you turn south at Pornichet and go to the resort of St Marc, it may look familiar, a sense of *déjà-vu,* explained by the fact that this is where Jacques Tati filmed that classic and hilarious comedy, *Monsieur Hulot's Holiday.*

Back on the coast road to St Nazaire an obelisk records that it was through this port that the first American troops of Pershing's Army landed in 1918, while, by the main jetty of the harbour, stands another obelisk, to the fallen of 'Operation Chariot', the great British Commando raid of 1942.

The object of the raid was to destroy the great graving dock, the *Forme-Ecluse,* the only dock on the French coast capable of receiving and repairing large German surface raiders. The force sent against the port consisted of No 2 Commando Unit and demolition parties from other commando units, the total raiding party consisting of 285 men. These men were carried in an old American Lease-lend exchange destroyer manned by the Royal Navy, HMS *Campbelltown,* and fourteen fast launches. The bows of HMS *Campbelltown* were crammed with high explosive and the idea was to ram the warship into the lockgate, land commandos to wreck installations and, after they had withdrawn on the launches, explode the vessel and so destroy the dock.

The force sailed up the river at 10pm on the night of 28 March, flying German ensigns and making suitable signals. They were nearing the docks before their true identity was discovered and the final run was made under heavy fire. The gates were rammed and the commandos landed to destroy much of the dockyard, but, this done, withdrawal was impossible. The defences were fully alerted and put the retreating launches through such a gauntlet of fire that only three managed to return to England. As dawn revealed the chaos of St Nazaire, the German garrison gradually rounded up the surviving commandos and snuffed out pockets of resistance.

Meanwhile, the *Campbelltown* remained jammed in the dock gates surrounded by a growing crowd of interested German soldiers, who eventually boarded her. There were nearly four-hundred troops there when at noon the ship blew up, destroying the gates and all on board. The St Nazaire raid was certainly 'the greatest raid of all', but the losses were severe. The Royal Navy lost 780 men, and the commandos 212 men out of their total landing force of 265, while many French people were killed in the fighting or in subsequent reprisals.

Nantes is the largest city in Brittany, the seventh in France, with a population of over a quarter of a million. Even for those who do not like large cities, Nantes is very agreeable. It has some interesting sights, such as the great Castle of the Dukes, some fine museums, scores of good restaurants and hotels for Breton and Vietnamese food, and, in the large network of pedestrian precincts, all the best shopping of France.

Nantes is a very ancient city, a capital of the Gaulish tribe, the *Namnetes,* hence Nantes, and was later a trading

Château de Nantes

centre for the Romans. During the time of the Dukes, and indeed right up until the time when this *département* was detached from the province, Nantes and Rennes debated their claims to be the capital of Brittany, and Nantes for size and style has to be declared the winner.

The castle was begun by Duke François II and completed by Duchesse Anne. It greatly impressed Henri IV when he arrived in the city and it was here that he signed the Edict of Nantes which granted religious toleration to the Protestants and ended, for a time at any rate, the Wars of Religion.

To visit Nantes, drive into the centre and park near the castle, off the Rue Henri IV. The main part of the city lies to the west, along the Cours Franklin Roosevelt, but the two great attractions of castle and cathedral are at hand and may be visited in a morning, while from

here the best way to see the city, (or indeed any city,) is to walk.

Nantes has always been a port and was once a slaving centre; cloth to Africa, slaves to the West Indies, with rum, sugar and spices carried on the return voyage. The slave merchants' houses still stand in the old part of the town, close to the river-port facilities; built from vast profits, very fine houses they are.

Like most castles, that in Nantes has had its vicissitudes serving as a palace, garrison and prison. Fouquet was arrested here and 'Bluebeard' Gilles de Rais was tried for his crimes in the castle hall and burned at the stake on the river bank nearby. Gilles had been a great soldier. He rode with Joan of Arc and became a Marshal of France, but he was more than a little mad, and after returning to his estates in the Vendée, he turned to witchcraft, necromancy and mass-murder, slaughtering children by the dozen, searching for the elixir of life, before he was finally arrested. The castle of Nantes is moated and its walls are tall. Inside is an excellent museum of Breton costume and furniture, including some fine *lit-clos,* cupboard-beds, and a maritime museum with relics of the slave trade.

From the castle it is a short walk to the cathedral of St Pierre. The exterior perhaps disappointing, is, in any case, being restored. The cathedral was built from about 1400, of limestone, not in the usual granite, a sparing example of Flamboyant Gothic, but with more than a touch of the pleasing Perpendicular. The vault of the nave is 120ft high and the clean lines of the pillars seem to make it far higher than that. The roof was destroyed by fire in 1972 and the restoration work is still in progress, but the interior is in excellent condition and uncluttered by excessive ornamentation. In one corner is the tomb of Duke François II and his wife Margarite of Foix. The side-niches of the tomb contain exquisite statues or 'weepers', including saints and martyrs and, most unusually, one of St Charlemagne, who was not even a cleric and by no means a saint.

All this part of the town is worth

General Cambronne

110

Cathedral of Saints Peter and Paul
Nantes
Recently restored, a very fine
example of the Gothic, with
interesting tombs.

Castle of the Dukes
Nantes
This contains several museums, open
every day except Tuesday. Guided
tours available.
    The Museum of Popular Art
    The Maritime Museum
    La Tour de La Couronne d'Or

Musée des Beaux-Arts
Nantes
A magnificent art gallery in the town
centre. Works by Courbet, Ingres, de
la Tour, etc.

Botanical Gardens
(Jardin des Plantes), Rue Baudrey
A very fine garden on the edge of the
city, close to the Gare d'Orleans.

exploring, and a little way along the Rue
Clemenceau is the Musée des Beaux
Arts, one of the finest provincial art
galleries in France. There are eighteen
galleries, with works by masters of all
periods, notably Georges de la Tour and
Ingres. The Spanish collection is
particularly fine.

In the centre of the town, the
botanical gardens have a statue of Jules
Verne, who was born here.

There is nothing to do here but
wander about, window-shopping, but
beyond the exquisite Place Royale, with
its fountain, is the Cours Cambronne,
with a statue of yet another prominent
Nantais, General Cambronne, who
commanded the infantry of the Old

Guard at Waterloo and sprang into the
history books on the strength of one
forceful phrase.

Exactly what the phrase was is still
disputed. The delicate and romantic say
that, when summoned to surrender by
the English he replied 'La Garde meurt,
mais ne se rend pas' best translated as
'The Guard knows how to die but not
how to surrender'. The more prosaic
believe he retorted simply *'Merde!'* The
first remark sounds like the sort one
would have wished to say, but thought
of later, while the second is far more
likely, and considerably more soldierly.

Nantes is fairly rich in native sons, for,
apart from Jules Verne and Cambronne,
there is Waldeck-Rousseau, the longest
reigning prime-minister of the Third
Republic; Lamoricière, a general of the
Algerian Wars who captured the Riff
leader, Abd-el-Kader; another notable
prime-minister, Briand; and, over the
ages, many dukes and princes.

Beyond the Cours Cambronne, down
by the riverine port, are many interesting
sights, and some fine old buildings,
especially along the quai de la Fosse.
Number 70 was once the capital of the
French East India Company, while
many of the others belonged to
merchants who grew rich from the
profits of the slave trade. Their houses
can be distinguished by their elegant
wrought-iron decoration on the window
grilles and gates.

From the Place l'Herminer up to the
Place Graslin, where at No 3
Cambronne died in 1842, are many little
shops and restaurants; Nantes food is
famous and very varied. La Cigogne in
the Rue Jean-Jacques Rousseau is
excellent, and you can avoid the
inevitable fish at Les Maraichers in the
Rue Fouré, and there are many other
excellent restaurants in the surrounding
countryside.

From Nantes, the traveller has a choice. He can return to St Nazaire to cross the Loire by the spectacular new bridge and visit the lands of the *pays de Retz,* or travel up the river, through the Muscadet country to the frontier of Brittany at Ancenis, or, finally, head north along the valley of the Erdré towards Châteaubriant, and so out of Loire-Atlantique altogether and into the Ile-et-Vilaine *département.*

Each route has its attractions and although now out of Brittany completely, the *pays de Retz* can hardly be ignored. It has some fine resorts, notably Pornic on the so-called Jade Coast, and the interesting island of Noirmoutier, where St Philibert established his mission to the savage pagan Gauls, returning through Machécoul, capital of the *pays de Retz,* with the donjon of Gilles de Rais' sinister castle. Inland the great castle at Clisson on the Sèvre, largely destroyed with the rest of the town in 1794, has imposing and picturesque remains.

North of Clisson, along the Sèvre, is the Muscadet country proper, and a chance to purchase a case or two directly from the *vignerons* before proceeding to Champtoceaux and Ancenis.

You can eat very well at the Voyageurs in Champtoceaux, walking off the effects afterwards by strolling along the promenade de Champalud.

From Nantes a river trip up the Erdre is a favourite Sunday excursion for the *Nantais* and the pleasure-craft are moored in rows along the banks north of the town. If you travel by car, it is wise to leave the *camion*-infested N137 as soon as possible, and travel instead by the minor roads from La Chapelle-sur-Erdre through Sucé, across the Nantes-Brest canal and so to Nort. From here it is a pleasant run to our last call in this *département,* the town of Châteaubriant.

Châteaubriant is in some ways a sad place. It is dominated by a huge castle, the ancestral home of the Lavals. When one Lord of Laval returned to his castle from the Crusades, his wife was so pleased to see him that she expired in his arms, which must have given that doughty knight quite a shock, but its later history is even less attractive. In the sixteenth century, the Count Jean married the beautiful Françoise de Foix and, knowing the king's reputation with the ladies, left his wife at home, when summoned to court by François the First.

The king heard of the count's beautiful wife, but when the count declined to produce her he discovered a signal by which the count could summon the lady. The king sent off the signal himself and to the count's rage, his wife duly appeared at court. Had the count stayed with his wife, all might have been well, but he stormed off home to Châteaubriant and left her behind, eventually to become the king's mistress.

When the king tired of her, she returned home to Châteaubriant, where the count kept her and her daughter imprisoned in a darkened room for ten years. The daughter soon died and, in the end, the count murdered his wife, a most unhappy lady.

GOOD BEACHES IN LOIRE ATLANTIQUE

St-Marc, near St-Nazaire
Le Croisic
La Baule

During World War II there was a prison camp outside Châteaubriant, used to confine suspected Resistance men and hostages taken by the Germans, and held against the good

Fougerès Castle

Coastline near Brest

Mont St Michel

behaviour of the populace.

Unfortunately, in October 1941, Colonel Holtz, commander of the garrison at Nantes, was ambushed and killed. As a reprisal, twenty-five men, some old, one only sixteen, were taken from the camp to a small quarry west of the town and shot. A further twenty-one were taken to Nantes and shot there. The execution site has become a place of pilgrimage, a stark memorial dominating the execution posts and studded with urns containing earth sent from every province of France by Maquis *réseau* as well as from the various concentration camps of the Third Reich. There is nothing even remotely beautiful about this site. It is a terrible place.

Châteaubriant *ville* is dominated by the great castle, which like most castles, was pulled down or remodelled several times and now largely dates from the late Renaissance. The keep is all that remains of the original medieval fortress and the buildings now contain a museum, the law courts, and the municipal offices.

The castle is imposing but the town seems depressed. From Châteaubriant our way is now north again for Rennes, to the present capital of the Province, and a visit to the frontier towns of the grand old Duchy.

9 Ille-et-Vilane: Brocéliande, Rennes, Fougères

The north-eastern *département* of Ille-et-Vilaine, full of interest and variety, contains many of the real gems the traveller seeks in the Breton countryside. This is truly a *département* crammed with curiosities. First, one should travel north-west from Châteaubriant, almost to the borders of the Morbihan, to the ancient and legendary forest of Brocéliande.

Brocéliande is not on any modern map. Today it is known as the forest of Paimpont, and echoes to the screech of saws and the crash of falling timber, but it is also a forest of romance and mystery, recognised as such for over two thousand years, and a place to approach with caution.

Brocéliande is a classic example of how, in Brittany, fact and legend are inextricably mixed. On the face of it, this is just a forest, one of the great medieval hunting grounds and preserved as such since ancient times. This particular forest, however, has gathered a great mass of legendary stories, appeared in ancient plays and *chansons de geste,* and offered magical potential from Druidic

The fountain of Baranton

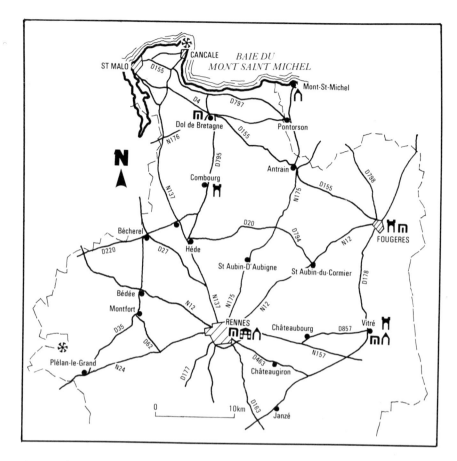

times to the present day.

Merlin, King Arthur's mentor and wizard, came to his end among these green acres. Merlin, who here appears as a young man rather than an old warlock with pointed hay and beard, was loved by the fairy Viviane, the Lady of the Lake, who was born in the château of Comper. Viviane, who had met King Arthur's knights before, afraid of losing Merlin, cast a spell upon him, and while he slept, encased him forever — some say inside an oak, others inside a stone. Some say — and even believe — that Merlin is still there, in the Val sans Retour, the Valley of No Return, near Trécesson, or that he is inside the Merlin

stone by the spring at Baranton.

To find the spring at Baranton is far from easy. Concoret is the largest place nearby and from there you travel through La Saudrais and turn off to the curiously-named hamlet of Folle-Pensée. At the far end of the village a sign points into the woods, stating positively, *'Fontaine de Baranton'*. The path is initially wide, then narrows, then dwindles, and finally disappears. Head south-west, on gradually rising ground and you may come to a place where small stones and rocks mark the route of an ancient path. Follow this, in a grove of oak trees is the fairy spring. It is contained in a deep granite basin, clear and cold water with a metallic taste. At the head of the basin, cast aside, and resembling an extra large kerb-stone, is the *perron de Merlin,* which is said on good historical evidence to have magical powers.

To summon rain take some water from the spring, sprinkle it on the stone and, within the hour clouds gather and the rain and hail comes down. This belief certainly dated from Druidic times, but processions came to the spring and invoked its aid as recently as 1935. In 1835, during a severe drought, the Vicar of Concoret led his congregation there, blessed the water and spinkled it on the stone, at which 'a violent thunderstorm arose and the rain fell with such violence that we hastened to disperse'.

These are just two of the legends of Brocéliande, but there are many more in the old Arthurian legends and subsequent folklore. Here, King Arthur's knights searched for the Holy Grail and here, Morgan le Fay (or Fée), the fairy, wove her plots.

The legend of Baranton's spring was certainly in existence as long ago as the fifth century and repeated almost exactly in Wace's *Roman de Rou,* written in about 1100.

Is it all true? Let Wace have the last word on it:

Not all lies, not all truth,
Not all fable, not all sooth.

Two final points. Reaching the fountain was difficult; the return is almost impossible. I was gloriously lost and had I not stumbled across a forester who led me out, I might be wandering there yet. When I told him that I had searched for the fountain and found it, he was amazed, 'You are very lucky' he said 'very few people have seen it'. Footsore and covered in mud, I did not feel very lucky.

Since Nantes has departed to join the Pays de La Loire, Rennes is the undoubted capital of Brittany. Even without this defection, Rennes has all the attributes of a capital, a university, a Palais de Justice, where the unfortunate Dreyfus was tried for the second time in 1899, and some fine public buildings. The nightlife is conspicuous by its absence, but the restaurants and hotels are very good; as a centre for touring Ille-et-Vilaine, Rennes has much to commend it.

The city is divided into two by the Vilaine, and driving is not rec-ommended. Drivers should abandon their cars at the station, give the hotel porter enough money to keep the meter fed, and explore the town on foot.

The old *quartier* of the town, always the most attractive part, is now a pedestrian precinct and lies south of the Palais du Commerce. The Rue St Georges is full of fine houses and has one good restaurant, Le Baron. The courtyards which lie behind these façades are full of interest. Each house has its interior courtyard, and you should probe these narrow alleyways to see what lies behind.

The cathedral of St Pierre is massive, and towers over the Place des Lices, the ancient *lists* or tournament ground, where Bertrand Duguesclin made his anonymous début in 1337, overthrowing one knight after another. He was so poor at the time that he had to borrow armour from one of his cousins and wearing borrowed armour was horribly uncomfortable, but in spite of this handicap he triumphed. Finally, Bertrand's visor was knocked open and his father, who had until then been more than a trifle ashamed of his ugly little son, rushed down to pound him on the back and promise him the finest armour

Rue St Georges, Rennes

La place du Palais, Rennes

that money could buy.

The medieval town was largely destroyed in the great fire of 1720, when the town burned for several days. The rebuilding was done on classical lines and the centre of the town is most attractive.

The Law Courts are a very ancient foundation. Rennes, the seat of the *Parlement* of Brittany since the days of

capitals, Rennes has art galleries,
concert halls, and an active artistic and
social life, largely centred on the
university. The townspeople claim that
for fun and frolic, Rennes leaves much
to be desired, but as a touring centre for
the visitor it is ideal.

To the west lies the frontier between
Brittany and France. Guarding the
approaches, therefore, is a series of
fortified towns and no traveller to
Brittany should fail to visit the greatest
fortresses of all, at Vitré and Fougères.

Vitré, to the east of Rennes, the
nearer, can be reached after side visits
to the ruins at Châteaugiron, and the
Fairy's Rock near La Guerche-de-
Bretagne. As you round the corner you
are confronted with the old houses, the
walls, the medieval gateways, and
the cobbled narrow streets leading up
into the old town. The château-fort
ramparts are huge, with a deep moat
spanned by a drawbridge. It dates from
the Hundred Years' War, but fell into
ruin and was purchased by the
municipality in 1820 for a mere 8,000
francs.

You can get a good view of the castle
from the banks of the little garden
opposite the Rue d'Embas. Off this lies
the Rue Beaudrairie, very medieval,
which leads uphill to the courtyard
facing the castle.

Below the north wall lies the suburb of
La Rachapt. This was seized by English
routiers, freebooters, during the
Hundred Years' War and, although the
castle remained in French hands, the
garrison felt uneasy with those
perfidious *Anglais* loafing about beneath
their feet, and eventually levied a large
enough bribe from the townspeople to
tempt the English to march away.
Rechapt is a corruption of the word
rechat, 're-purchase'. This suburb later
became a hotbed of Calvinism during

the Duchesse Anne, has consistently
maintained the rights of the duchy
against the encroachments of King and
Paris. The magnificent council chambers
remain, and can be visited. Like all good

Palais du Parlimrnt, Rennes

the Wars of Religion, when the town belonged to the unfortunate Coligny family.

The streets of the town are full of interest and on one wall of the church of Notre Dame is an outside pulpit, used firstly to preach to the townsfolk and later, in Coligny's day, by the Catholic priests to argue doctinal points with Protestant pastors in the house opposite. Vitré is a fine place, certainly one of the most interesting towns of France for the medievalist. On the road north, stop on the *Tertres Noirs,* a small hill just outside the town and look back from there. As the sun goes down, the walls and shadows of Vitré look black and formidable against the sky.

Fougères grows on you. This is the Breton town which appears on all the posters, but when you arrive, and are carried into the town on a tidal wave of traffic, it can be a little alarming.

However, it improves. The pearl of Fougères is not the town, but the castle, and this lies below and beyond the town itself. Some castle-builders preferred hill-sites, but others preferred the valleys where they could divert some river into an impassable moat, and so it is with Fougères. A walk round the walls of the castle reveals military architecture at its finest. There are high walls built on rock and screened by the moat. Scaling these walls, even today, unopposed, would be a task indeed. In fact, although the town on the hill is one of those places which was damaged during World War II, the

Fairy Rock, Ille et Vilaine

Vitré

castle has survived seven hundred years
of conflict remarkably well.

The first castle on this site was built
before the Conquest, but it fell to Henry
II Plantagenet, in 1166, when he was
invading the Duchy to advance the
claims of his son Geoffrey, and levelled
this castle to the ground. The present
castle was begun shortly afterwards,
although the first of the present towers
was erected only in the fourteenth
century. The castle was besieged
incessantly during the Hundred Years'
War and changed hands several times.
The best view of the castle is from the
lower water gate, near the castle mill and
from here the castle runs off, along the
spur, and encloses a large parkland. One
can visit the castle and walk along the

ramparts inside, looking out on town
and *bourg,* a really evocative way to visit
this doughty fortress.

Fourgères *ville* is less inspiring, but
quite agreeable. There is a good view
over the castle from the public gardens,
the Place des Arbres, while the Lion
d'Or is a good place to stay, especially if
you dine at the Restaurant St Pierre next
door.

North-east from Fougères is the island
monastery of Mont-St-Michel. Whether
Mont-St-Michel lies in Brittany or
Normandy, depends entirely on the
course of the river Couesnon, which
historically marked the frontier between
the two great duchies and runs around
the island. The river, backed up along its
course by the fierce tides of the bay has

Château at Vitré

Château at Fougères

changed course frequently and for the moment places this spectacular site firmly in Normandy, but only just.

It is advisable, if possible, to visit Mont-St-Michel out of season, preferably in the early spring or late autumn. In November, on a grey cold day, when the normally crowded streets are empty and even Mère Poulard's restaurant is taking its annual *congé*, a chill wind can sweep round every corner and the monstery, quite deserted, seems almost haunted. It is easy to get lost here and wander around for a long time, heaving open heavy oak doors and climbing up and down endless flights of steps before emerging on the great terrace. From this windy platform, the bay below is spectacular, the tide sweeping in with a series of tall waves, crashing over into foam and white crests. They say that the tide sweeps into St Michel's Bay at the speed of a galloping horse, a fearsome sight, even from a safe vantage point 300ft above the waves.

The abbey was begun in the eighth century and is dedicated to the Archangel Michael, who fought a duel with the Devil on nearby Mont Dol and afterwards directed the Bishop of Avranches to build a chantry chapel on the lonely island in the bay to keep the Devil away. This chapel, much altered, still stands as a place of pilgrimage and now contains a large silver statue of the saint.

In later centuries the island became a monastery, a fortress and a prison, and eventually, given the glorious site, a tourist trap. It must not be missed, however, and no visitor should leave without visiting the Restaurant de La Mère Poulard, and having one of their

Chapel, Dol de Bretagne

Château de Combourg

huge, feathery omelettes. These are large dishes, each as big as a soup plate, frothing inside and puffing jets of steam as the waiter slides it on to your plate.

You should try to arrive at sunset, when the westering sun sweeps down out of the sky and fills the bay with shadows. Then you can regain the mainland by the

causeway and dine very comfortably at the Hôtel au Bon Accueil on the road to Pontorson.

Our road lies to the west now, on the last lap back to St Malo and the ferry home, but Brittany has a strong grip and will not willingly let go. You can, if you have time to spare, walk down the valley of the Cousenon, on that entrancing footpath, the GR39, which leads south, past Tramblay and eventually, after

some sixty miles, to the capital at Rennes, or stroll into Normandy along the coast, for Brittany is full of footpaths, especially those waymarked trails of the *Comité National des Sentiers de Grande Randonneé* and, with plenty of campsites available for overnight stops, the whole province is a walker's paradise in whatever area you choose to roam.

We must go west, however, across the reclaimed 'polders' around Mont-St-

Michel, and so up to Mont Dol, and the nearby town of Dol-de-Bretagne. Mont Dol, which dominates this flat hinterland, was once, like Mont-St-Michel, an island. It is a granite knoll, some 200ft in height and now a pilgrim centre, a mixture of little chapels and ruined windmills.

You can see Mont-St-Michel from Mont Dol and inspect, stamped in the rock there, the footprints of St Michel, for it is here that he fought hand in hand with the Devil. It is said that before the fight St Michel was on his mount out in the bay and leapt across to Mont-Dol to accept the Devil's challenge.

The land between the two islands has been steadily drained since the thirteenth century and is now much used as grazing land for sheep. They provide the basis for that delicious tangy mutton, *pre-sale,* from the salt-fields. Dol itself is a little place with the usual quaint collection of old houses and at least one excellent restaurant, the Bretagne.

South of Dol lies the great castle of Combourg, home of René de Châteaubriand and this large and gloomy castle provided some of the grimmer passages in his *Mémoires d'Outre-Tombe.* At the time the family lived there, money was in short supply and René spent much of the time in his draughty bedroom, plagued by fears of ghosts and listening fearfully to the wind moaning round the towers. Even today, Combourg, swathed in tall trees, is hardly a jaunty castle, but it is admittedly imposing, especially when seen from across the park on the minor road which leads towards Cancale.

Cancale is *the* oyster port, and a very attractive place to visit. This is the gateway to the Côte d'Emeraude, and solely devoted to the oyster, growing, garnering and eating it in vast amounts. The oyster beds lie out in the bay and scores of boats go out at each ebb, to gather in the harvest. Most of the catch is cleaned and consumed in the hotels and restaurants behind the beach. The bay contains the three main types of oyster, the large *cancales,* the *bélons,* and the little *portugaises.* For a sea food feast, do not leave before eating at least once at Le Cancalais on the quai Gambetta.

On the final tour, go out to the Pointe du Grouin, and follow the *corniche* route along the coast, for even here, at the last minute, the duchy will surprise you with still more secret coves and sudden stretches of golden sands swept by the green sea, before you come through Rotheneuf, and the hotels of Paramé, and so into the town of St Malo, behind the Inter-muros.

Brittany has always been a popular province with the British, and for many reasons they feel very much at home there. It is a gentle place, where only the coastline is dramatic, but the region has so much to see and there is so much to do that those who go there once are sure to return, again and again.

Something should always be kept for the end, and dinner at L'Abordage in the Place de la Poissonnerie will keep your spirits up on the final evening until, with the following day, the bright ferry comes round the Grande Bé, and takes you back home to your own island.

Further Information For Visitors

Listed alphabetically by nearest town.

The Chârtreuse d'Auray
Auray
Open: daily 10-11.30am, 2.30-5pm.

Combourg
Open: Easter-September, 2-6pm (except Tuesday).

Fougères Castle
Guided tours only at: 10am, 11am, 2pm and 5pm. Also 4pm, 5pm and 6pm in summer. Closed January.

Hotel-Dieu
Guingamp
A medieval hospital.

Josselin Castle
Open: June - mid-September, 2-5pm.

Kergrist Castle
Lannion
(Exterior only)

Rosanbo Castle
West of Lanvellec.

Kerjean Castle
West of Morlaix.

Beauport Abbey
Paimpol
Open: Easter-Whitsun, June-September, 9am-12 noon, 2-7pm.

Law Courts
Rennes
Open: all day except 12 noon-2pm.

Château de la Bretesche
St Guildas
Open: 10am-12 noon, 2-4pm.

Fort La Latte
Cap Fréhel, west of St Malo
Open: Easter, Whitsun, June-October, 9am-6.30pm.

Quic-en-Groigne Tower
St Malo Inter-Muros
Open: Easter - mid-September, 9am-12 noon, 1.30-7pm.

Tonquedec Castle
On D31, south of Lannion

Listed alphabetically by town.

Musée Historique de Belle-Ile
Le Palais, Belle Ile

Fine Arts Museum
Rue Emile Zola, Brest
Paintings, sacred sculpture.

J. Miln-Le-Rouzic Prehistory Museum
Carnac
Open: daily in summer, 8am-12 noon, 1-7pm.
Prehistoric archaeology.

Fishing Museum
Concarneau

Castle Museum
Dinan
Open: 10am-12 noon, 2-6pm.
Regional costumes, weapons, furniture,
fossils, archaeology, textile industry.

Sea Museum
17 Ave Georges V, Dinard
Personal objects of the explorer
Charcot.

La Guillotière Museum
Dol-de-Bretagne

Fougères Castle
(Inner tower and Gobelin tower - see
Castles for times of guided tours.)

Musée de Guérande
Guérande
Open: Easter-October, 9am-12 noon,
2-7pm.

Mathurin Méheut Museum
Maison du Bourreau, Lamballe

Museum of the Compagnie des Indes
Lorient

Musée des Jacobins
Rue des Vignes, Morlaix
Open: 10am-12 noon, 2-6pm (except
Tuesday).
Archaeology, sacred art, Breton
furniture, paintings.

Castle of the Dukes of Brittany
Nantes
Various museums:
   The Museum of Popular Art
   The Maritime Museum
   La Tour de La Couronne d'Or
Open: 10am-12 noon, 2-6pm, daily
(except Tuesday).

Musée des Beaux-Arts
Nantes

Museum of Art and Archaeology
Nantes

Gauguin Museum
Town Hall, Pont Aven
Open: 10am-12 noon, 2-6pm.

Musée Bigouden
Château, Pont l'Abbé
Open: 10am-12 noon, 2-5pm.
Local costumes, furniture, utensils, sea
faring.

Atlantic Museum
Citadel, Port Louis
Huge sea museum to Battle of Atlantic
1940-4.

War Museum
Citadel, Port Louis
In the former powder magazine.

Ship Museum
Port Louis
Includes three-masted barque.

Fine Arts Museum
10 Place St Coventin, Quimper.
Paintings, including Pont Aven
Impressionists and Max Jacob rooms.

Breton Folklore Museum
Ancien Evêché, Rue du Roi Gradlon,
Quimper
Archaeology, furniture, local costumes,
pottery.

La Grande Maison
Rte de Benodet, Quimper
Private pottery museum.

Fine Arts Museum (Musée des Beaux Arts)
Quai Emile Zola, Rennes
Open: 10am-12 noon, 2-6pm (except Tuesday).
Egyptian, Greek and Roman antiquities, paintings, drawings, pottery.

Bicton Museum
Rennes

Brittany Museum
Quai Emil Zola, Rennes
History of Brittany from prehistoric times to present day, furniture, costumes, crafts, traditions.

Breton Car Museum
Rennes

Town Museum
Castle, St Malo
History of the town and its famous men, privateering, fishing, shipbuilding.

Cape Horner Museum
Tour Solidor, St Malo
History of voyages round the world and sailing ship, models, maps, pictures.

Musée Ernest Renan
20 Rue Ernest Renan, Tréguier

Prehistoric Museum
Rue Noë, Vannes
Open: 9.30am-12 noon, 2-6pm (except Sunday).
Prehistoric, Gallo-Roman and medieval finds.

Musée de Vitré
Castle, Vitré
Open: 10am-12 noon, 2-5pm (except Tuesday).
Wood carvings, furniture, tapestries, pottery.

RESTAURANTS

There are many restaurants in Brittany; the following (listed alphabetically by the town) is a selection of those recommended by the author.

Le Goyen,
Place Jean Simon, Audierne.
Tel: (98) 70 08 88

Jeanne d'Arc,
52 Rue de la Plage, St Marine, Benodet.
Tel: (98) 56 32 70

Le Frère Jacques,
15 Rue de Lyon, Brest.
Tel: (98) 44 38 65

Castel Régis,
Plage du Garo, Brignogan-Plage.
Tel: (98) 83 40 22

Le Cancalais,
Quai Gambetta, Cancale.
Tel: (99) 89 61 93

Restaurant de Bricourt,
rue Duguesclin, Cancale.
Tel: (99) 89 64 76

Lann-Roz,
Ave de la Poste, Carnac.
Tel: (97) 52 10 48

Le Galion,
Ville Close, 15 Rue Guénole,
Concarneau.
Tel: (98) 97 30 16

L'Avaugour,
1 Place du Guesclin, Dinan.
Tel: (96) 39 07 49

La Caravelle,
14 Place Duclos, Dinan.
Tel: (96) 39 00 11

Restaurant Altair,
18 Bvd Féart, Dinard.
Tel: (99) 46 13 58

Le Petit Robinson,
La Richardais, Dinard.
Tel: (99) 46 14 82

La Collegiale,
Faubourg Bizienne, Guérande.
Tel: (40) 24 97 29

Château de Locguenole,
(on D781), Hennebont.
Tel: (97) 76 29 04

Hotel du Château,
Rue General-de-Gaulle, Josselin.
Tel: (97) 22 20 11

L'Espadon,
2 Ave de la Plage, La Baule.
Tel: (40) 60 05 63

Beau Rivage,
Plage de Toulhors, Lamour-Plage.
Tel: (97) 65 50 11

Le Clos du Pontic,
Rue du Pontic, Landerneau.
Tel: (98) 21 50 91

Auberge Bretonne,
Place du Guesclin, La Roche-Bernard.
Tel: (99) 90 60 28

Auberge des Deux Magots,
Place du Bouffay, La-Roche-Bernard.
Tel: (99) 60 75

L'Estacade,
4 Quai Lénigo, Le Croisic.
Tel: (40) 23 03 77

La Voile d'Or,
La Plage, Le Pouliguen.
Tel: (40) 42 31 68

Manoir de Moellien,
Plovenez-Porzay, Locronon.
Tel: (98) 92 50 40

La Bretagne,
6 Place de la Liberation, Lorient.
Tel: (97) 64 34 65

Le Poisson d'Or,
1 Rue Maitre-Esvelin, Lorient.
Tel: (97) 21 57 06

La Sirène,
4 Rue Kerregan, Nantes.
Tel: (40) 47 00 17

L'Esquinade,
7 Rue St Denis, Nantes.
Tel: (40) 48 17 22

Relais Brenner,
Pont de Lezardieux, Paimpol.
Tel: (96) 20 11 05

Le Homard Bleu,
Plage de Trestraou, Bvd Joseph-le-Bihan,
Peros Guirec.
Tel: (96) 23 24 55

Au Char-a-Bancs,
Moulin de la Ville Geffroy, Plelo.
Tel: (96) 74 13 63

Relais du Val d'Oust,
Plöermel.
Tel: (97) 74 94 33

Le Barbie,
La Point de l'Arcouest, Ploubazlanec.
Tel: (96) 20 92 15

Hotel des Voyageurs,
6 Quai St Laurent, Ploudalmezeau.
Tel: (98) 87 00 37

Auberge de Kernank,
Route de Quiberon, Plouharnel.
Tel: (97) 52 01 41

Les Rochers,
Rue du Port, Ploumanach.
Tel: (96) 23 23 02

Hotel Robic,
Rue Jean-Jaures, Pontivy.
Tel: (97) 25 11 80

Avel-Vor,
Rue Locmalo, Port Louis.
Tel: (97) 82 47 59

La Bretagne,
Rue St Michel, Questembert.
Tel: (97) 26 11 12

La Petite Sirene,
Bvd de la Mer, Quiberon.
Tel: (97) 50 17 34

Les Tritons,
Allées de Locmaria, Quimper.
Tel: (98) 90 61 78

Le Relais du Roch,
(On D49), Quimperlé.
Tel: (98) 96 12 97

Hotel Lion d'Or,
Grande Rue, Rochefort-en-Terre.
Tel: (97) 43 32 80

Ar Maner,
Bvd Ste-Barbe, Roscoff.
Tel: (98) 69 70 78

Gulf Stream,
Rue Marquise de Kergeriou, Roscoff.

L'Aiguade,
46-48 Rue de Gouet, Saint-Brieuc.
Tel: (96) 33 56 44

L'Abordage,
pl de la Poissonnerie, St Malo.
Tel: (99) 40 87 53

Duchesse Anne,
pl Guy La Chambre, St Malo.
Tel: (99) 40 85 33

La Porte St-Pierre,
2 Place du Guet, St Malo.
Tel: (99) 40 91 27

La Metairie de Beauregard,
St Etienne, St Servan.
Tel: (99) 81 37 06

Ti-Al-Lannec,
Allée de Mezo-Guen, Trebeurden.
Tel: (96) 23 57 26

Le Roof,
Presqu'ile de Conleau, Vannes.
Tel: (97) 63 47 47

L'image Ste Anne,
8 Place de la Liberation, Vannes.
Tel: (97) 63 27 36

La Maree Bleue,
Place Bir Hakeim, Vannes.
Tel: (97) 47 24 29

Petit-Billot,
pl Marechal Le Clerc, Vitré.
Tel: (99) 75 02 10

GOLF COURSES

18-hole unless specified otherwise.

Golf de Dinard,
Dinard-St-Briac.
Tel: (99) 88 32 07

Hôtel du Golf de la Bretesche,
La Bretesche.
Tel: (40) 45 30 05

Golf de Quimper et de Gornouaille,
Manoir de Mesmeur,
La Forêt Fouesnant. (9-hole)
Tel: (98) 56 02 02

Golf de Lann Rohou,
Landerneau.
Tel: (98) 85 16 17

Golf des Adjoncs d'Or,
Lantic.
Tel: (96) 70 48 13

Golf de St Laurent,
Plöermel.
Tel: (97) 24 31 72

Golf de St Samson,
Pleumer-Bodou.
Tel: (96) 23 87 34

Golf de St Jacques de la Lande,
Rennes- (9-hole)
Tel: (99) 64 24 18

Golf de Sables d'Or les Pins,
Sables d'Or-Fréhel. (9-hole)
Tel: (96) 41 42 57

Golf de Pen-Guen,
St-Cast-le-Guildo.
(9-hole)
Tel: (96) 41 03 20

MEGALITHIC REMAINS IN BRITTANY

Menhirs
Standing stones, often found alone, but
also in large numbers. There are three
thousand at Carnac, one thousand at
Erdeven, others at St Just in Ille-et-
Vilaine.

Dolmens
Burial chambers are found in Finistère
and in Morbihan, notably at
Loqmariaquer.

Roofed Galleries
Several of these are found in Brittany,
notably the Roche aux Feés (Fairy
Rock) in Ille-et-Vilaine, and the Mougo
at Commance in Finistère.

CASINOS

Casinos, with gambling and discos, are
found in the following Breton towns:

Perros-Guirec
Bénodet
Dinard
St Malo
Quiberon
Pléneuf-Val-André

WALKING IN BRITTANY

Brittany is well supplied with footpaths
including a number of the great long-
distance footpaths of the Grande
Randonnée:

GR37	Sillé-le-Guillaume to Vitré
GR37	Vitré to Dinan
GR37	Dinan to Josselin
GR37	Josselin to Huelgoat
GR34	Huelgoat to Douarnenez
GR347	Josselin to Redon
GR39	Rennes to Mont-St-Michel
GR380	Morlaix to Huelgoat

Full details on walking, cycling,
camping and gites d'etape can be
obtained from:
ABRI (Association Bretonne des Relais
    et Itineraires),
3 Rue des Portes - Mordelaises,
3500 Rennes.
Tel: (99) 79 36 26

The French Government Tourist Office,
178 Piccadilly,
London W1V 0AL
Tel: 01 491 7622

French Government Tourist Office
610 5th Avenue
New York, New York

Maison de la Bretagne,
Central Commercial Maine-
    Montparnasse,
17 Rue de l'Arrivée,
Paris, Cedex 15.
Tel: (1) 538 73 15

Paris Tourist Office,
Bureau d'accueil Central,
127 av. des Champs-Elysées - 75008.
Telephone: Paris 723 61 72

In Brittany
Comité Regional au Tourisme,
3 Rue d'Espagne,
BP 2275,
Rennes.
Tel: (99) 50 11 15

Local information can be obtained from
Tourist Offices *(Syndicate d'Initiative),*
found in all towns and most villages.

TRAVELLING IN FRANCE

By Car
Driving:
    Keep to the right, overtaking on the
    left. Beware *'priorité a droit'* in towns.
    Drivers coming from the right, have
    right of way.

Speed limits:
    Built up areas 60km/h (37mph)
    unless otherwise indicated.
    Outside built up areas 90km/h
    (56mph) unless otherwise indicated.
    By-pass motorways 110 km/h
    (68mph).
    Dual carriageway roads with central
    reserve 110 km/h (68mph).
    Inter-urban motorways 130km/h
    (80mph).

Lighting:
    From dusk to sunrise use dipped
    headlights in built up areas.

Compulsory accessories:
    Spare bulbs for headlights, safety
    lock on doors, left hand driving
    mirror, advance warning signal (tri-
    angle).

Hooting:
    Between dusk and dawn use flashing
    headlights if it is necessary to warn
    other road users, only use your horn
    in an emergency.

Crash Helmets:
    Compulsory for both rider and
    passengers of all types of motorcycles
    inside and outside built up areas.

Seat belts:
    Compulsory everywhere and in no
    case may children under-10 years old
    sit in the front of a vehicle.

Fines:
    Drivers that are liable for a fine and
    cannot show proof of an address or
    of employment within French
    territory must pay immediately on
    demand, the police will provide a
    receipt.

Roads:
France has a road network covering a total of about 930,000 miles, including 3,000 miles of motorway. Maintenance is excellent on minor 'D' roads which offer the advantage of less traffic and beautiful country.

Car hire:
The CSNCRA (Chambre Syndicate Nationale de Commerce et de la Réparation Automobile) publishes a directory of those of its members who run a car hire service (all makes). CSNCRA: 6 rue Léonardo-de-Vinci, Paris.

By Train

The French railway network, SNCF, offers various ways of safe inexpensive travel.
N.B. All rail tickets must be '*composted*' — pre-stamped before boarding train. There are 'composter' machines at every platform entrance.

1 'France Vacances' — pass entitles unlimited travel all over France. Details from travel agents or from any French Railways office abroad.

2 'Train + Auto' — 200 stations providing a self-drive car to await your arrival. Details from the Central booking office in Paris, telephone 292 02 92 or information leaflets from any railway station.

3 'Train Autos Couchettes, (Car sleeper trains).

4 'Train + Vélo' — service for cyclists Over 100 stations at which a cycle for use in the town for rides in the country may be booked. See 'Train + Vélo' leaflet from travel agents or French railway stations.

Further information from:
SNCF French Railways Ltd,
179 Piccadilly, London W1X 0BA
Telephone: 01-493-4451

By Air
Internal:
AIR FRANCE is the national airline running daily flights to 30 towns in France. An extensive system of reduced rates for all passengers may bring your fare down by nearly 60%.
For all particulars: contact Air France (Georgian House, 69 Boston Manor Road, Brentford, Middlesex. Telephone: 01-568-4411 or 666 5th Avenue, New York, New York), or your own travel agency. C.T.A.R. (Comté des Transporteurs Aériens Régionaux) represents ten regional air lines.
All particulars from: 15 Square Max-Hymans, 75741 Paris Cedex 15. Telephone 5671265

There are regular flights from Paris to Rennes, Dinard, Saint-Brieuc, Lannion, Brest, Quimper, Lorient and Nantes.

ACCOMMODATION

Hotels
Hôtels de Tourisme are divided into categories according to quality of accommodation and standard of service and are identified by the number of stars.
***** L Palatial de luxe establishment
****
***
**
* *Ordinary tourist hotel with adequate amenities*

Motel de Tourisme marked 'M' are classified in accordance with the same criteria as the hotels.

Relais de Tourisme are hotels with a smaller number of rooms which cater for visitors desirous of enjoying a more elaborate cuisine. They are marked 'R.T.'.

Les Logis de France are small or medium hotels meeting a specific code of requirements, generally in the 1 and 2 star class.

Youth Hostels

There are many youth hostels in Brittany.

Further details can be obtained from:
YHA, Trevelyan House,
8 St Stephen's Hill,
St Albans, Herts AL1 2DY England
Telephone: St Albans 55215

American Youth Hostels Association
75 Spring Street,
New York, New York

Fédération Unie des Auberges
de Jeunesse,
6 rue Mesnil, 751165 Paris
Telephone: 2855540

la ville - town
le village - village
le bâtiment municipal - public building
la mairie - town hall
les environs - surrounding country
habiter - to live in
le jardin public - park
la rue - road
le boulevard - broad street
le boulevard périphérique - ring road
le trottoir - pavement, sidewalk
le passage clouté - pedestrian crossing
la station service - petrol filling station
l'essence - petrol

le chemin de fer - railway
la gare - station
le guichet - booking office
le billet simple - single ticket
le billet d'aller et retour - return ticket
le quai - platform
le consigne - left-luggage office
l'aéroport - airport
par avion - by air, by plane

le courrier - the mail
la carte postale - postcard
le timbre - (postage) stamp
la boîte aux lettres - letter box
la caisse - cashiers office, cash desk
toucher un chèque - to cash a cheque
la banque - bank

la magasin - shop
le cliente - customer
à bas prix - low priced
le comptoir - counter
le supermaché - supermarket
l'épicier - grocer
le boucher - butcher

la ferme - farm
le vigneron - wine grower
le raisin - grape
le vendanges - grape-harvest
champ - field

l'église - church
la cathédrale - cathedral
la chapelle - chapel
l'abbaye - abbey
l'école - school
pont - bridge
rivière - river

sortie - way out
en - in
poussée - push
tirage - pull
droite - right
gauche - left

Bibliography

Brittany, Henry Myhill, (Faber & Faber, 1964)

Early Brittany, Nora Chadwick, (University of Wales Press, 1969)

Oyster River, George Millar, (Bodley Head, 1963)

Brittany, A.H. Broderick, (Hodder & Stoughton, 1951)

Brittany and the Bretons, Keith Spence, (Gollancz, 1978)

Brittany Roundabout, Garry Hogg, (Museum Press, 1953)

La Bretagne et du Maine, (Total Guide, 1975)

Gault Millau Guide de la France, (current edition)

Brittany (Green Michelin Guide)

Guide Michelin

Guide des Auberges et Logis de France, (current edition)

Brittany, Brian Jackman and Margaret Hides, (Sunday Times, 1975)

The Devil's Brood, Alfred Duggan, (Transworld, 1977)

Ducal Brittany 1364-1399, Michael Jones, (OUP, 1970)

Index

PL
4-90

DATE DUE

MAY 2 9 1990			
JAN 2 2 1991			
JUN 0 3 1991			
APR 1 4 1994			

HIGHSMITH   45230